THE SOVIET VIEW
OF THE INDONESIAN
REVOLUTION

RUTH T. McVEY

THE SOVIET VIEW
OF THE INDONESIAN
REVOLUTION

A Study in the Russian Attitude Towards Asian Nationalism

EQUINOX
PUBLISHING
JAKARTA KUALA LUMPUR

Equinox Publishing (Asia) Pte Ltd
No 3. Shenton Way
#10-05 Shenton House
Singapore 068805

www.EquinoxPublishing.com

The Soviet View of the Indonesian Revolution
A Study in the Russian Attitude Towards Asian Nationalism
by Ruth T. McVey

ISBN 978-602-8397-07-0

First Equinox Edition 2009

1 3 5 7 9 10 8 6 4 2

Cornell Modern Indonesian Project Interim Reports
This title was originally published as an "Interim Report" in the Cornell Modern Indonesia Project (CMIP) series organized by the Cornell Southeast Asia Program. CMIP's first "Interim Report" appeared in 1956, during an era when little scholarship on Indonesia was available, and those studies that did appear often lagged far behind the actual events taking place in the country. George Kahin, director of CMIP at the time, explained in his foreword to the first "Interim Report" that these books were intended to address this lack of timely scholarship and encourage lively critical exchanges among researchers and readers. Therefore, as he explained, the "Interim Reports" would be "explicitly tentative and provisional in character." We believe that an understanding of this historical context is key to a full appreciation of these contributions to the study of Indonesia in the twentieth century.

PREFACE

Although in recent years there have been an increasing number of studies of the Indonesian Communist Party and of the Indonesian revolution (1945-49), there has been relatively little attention paid specifically to the role of the party in the revolutionary period and its relationship during that period with the Soviet Union. Furthermore, virtually no studies have been made of the perceptions of the Soviet Union of the character of the Indonesian revolution and the level of sophistication and understanding which its Indonesian specialists brought to the study of Indonesian affairs of this period. We believe that with this *Interim Report* Ruth McVey has made an important beginning in overcoming our ignorance of this most important subject. Her study makes a significant contribution both to our understanding of Indonesian Communism and of Soviet relations with Asian Communist parties in the critical period after World War II.

From 1954 to 1956, Miss McVey undertook intensive research on Soviet materials available in the United States and Western Europe and on Dutch Communist and Indonesian Communist publications available in the Netherlands and at Cornell. This study, first published in 1957, is based on her analysis of these documents and covers the period 1945-1950.

Miss McVey received her M.A. in 1954 from the Harvard Soviet Area Program. Subsequently under the auspices of the Cornell Modern Indonesia Project she carried on research for fifteen months in the Netherlands and England, and it was following this that she wrote this *Interim Report*. After further graduate work at Cornell, Miss McVey was awarded a Ford Foundation fellowship for additional research in the Netherlands and Indonesia. She received her Ph.D. from Cornell University in 1961.

Continuing demand for Miss McVey's study has led the Cornell Modern Indonesia Project to issue this Third Printing.

ITHACA, NEW YORK   George McT. Kahin
November 15, 1969   Director

TABLE OF CONTENTS

INTRODUCTION

We in the West, nervously observing current Soviet overtures to uncommitted Asia, tend sometimes to forget that the Communist path in the East has not always been a straight and purposeful one and that it has been marked by inconsistencies at least as great as those manifested by American policy in that part of the world. For the USSR has found it no easy task to make the choice with which it has generally been faced in its Asian dealings: whether to sacrifice local Communist interests in an attempt to gain the friendship of the nationalist movement, or to push Communist efforts to gain power at the risk of alienating Asian nationalism.

This study is an attempt to trace the Soviet attitude towards one manifestation of Asian nationalism — the Indonesian revolt against Netherlands rule — in an effort to show the development of Soviet thought on this problem in the opening years of the cold war. As such, it will restrict itself largely to Soviet doctrine and will avoid, wherever possible, a discussion of Indonesian domestic politics of the time. The reader should therefore bear in mind that a greatly over-simplified view of the Indonesian political scene is presented here, and that this paper is in no way a guide for developments in that sphere. It should also be noted that the Left referred to here is the political grouping which came to identify itself with the international Communist line; but the term has little meaning beyond this, for Indonesian politics cannot be neatly divided into a pro-Soviet Left and an anti-Soviet Right.

This *caveat* in mind, we shall turn back a decade to the end of the Second World War, when, amid the myriad other problems of that troubled moment, the Soviet Union found itself faced with the task of adopting a policy towards the rising wave of Asian nationalism. For some ten years, except for the brief period of Nazi-Soviet friendship, the USSR had urged an extremely moderate program in the East, calling for cooperation with the colonial powers against the greater danger of fascism. Now the Axis threat to Soviet existence had been removed. Should the moderate course continue to be pursued, and if so to what degree? Should there be cooperation with the non-communist ("bourgeois") nationalists, and if so on what basis? How much should events in Europe be allowed to determine the Communist attitude in Asia?

Soviet experience in the pre-war period did little to answer these questions. Before the Second World War, the Comintern had responded to the colonial problem in one of two ways, which had been applied Largely in reflection of Soviet policies in Europe. The first of these was the "united front from above." This strategy, first outlined by Lenin at the second Comintern congress in 1920, envisaged Communist collaboration with the leadership of non-communist movements for purposes considered common to the interests of both. In the Asian situation, this policy meant Communist support of bourgeois nationalist movements against the imperialist powers. It was not felt necessary that the Communists lead the cooperative venture, although usually political differences between the two groups were so wide as to result in disagreement and a subsequent struggle for power. This policy reached its most extreme development during the Chinese resolution of the 1920's in the theory of the "bloc within." At that time, on the argument that the Kuomintang represented an anti-imperialist bloc of workers, peasants, and petty and middle bourgeoisie, the Chinese Communists entered that movement and gave it their complete support.

The second strategy, that of the "united front from below," was adopted by the sixth Comintern congress in 1928, at which time the communist attitude towards non-communist movements underwent a thorough revision. The bourgeois nationalists were now considered to have sold out to imperialism, and it was declared that the only true representatives of the national liberation movement were the Communists themselves. Cooperation with non-communist nationalist movements was therefore abandoned, and efforts were made to win away their following. In general, this policy tended to rely more on the urban proletariat and less on the peasantry and on nationalist sentiment; it was more radical, though not necessarily more violent. The unread front from below was followed until the Comintern's adoption of the Popular Front in 1935 heralded not only a return to cooperation with non-communists but even collaboration with the colonial powers.[1]

The use of these alternative policies by the Communist parties was, as we have already mentioned, largely a reflection of Soviet policies in Europe. Even in China, where Soviet interest was considerable in the 1920's, the Russian attitude was determined more by events in Europe and by the Stalin-Trotsky feud than by the situation in China itself. In spite of the frequently-expressed Leninist claim that the capitalist chain would break at its weakest link — the areas under imperialist oppression — the USSR saw Europe as the main area of its diplomatic and ideological concern. As for the Comintern's policies in Asia, they met with almost complete defeat. The colonial governments were still too powerful and had no mind to tolerate Communism; while in countries like Turkey and China, where nationalist revolutions did take place, the nationalists used the Communists for their own ends and then disposed of them. Stalin had claimed the Communists would squeeze the Kuomintang like a lemon and then throw it away: but it was the other way round in reality. No since the failure of the Comintern in the Chinese revolution had a Soviet-directed Asian Communist party played a role of even minor political importance for the Soviet Union. In view of this manifest failure, it is small wonder that the USSR did not step forward at the end of the war with a clearcut Asian policy.

---

[1]   For an excellent discussion of these policies see John H. Kautsky, *Moscow and the Communist Party of India*, Cambridge, 1954, pp. 8-14.

1945: HESITATION

August 17, 1945: Indonesia, under Japanese occupation since 1942, declared its independence from Dutch colonial rule. In the months following this action, the new republic remained largely cut off from the rest of the world. Only the Dutch had any degree of knowledge about the situation there; and they, not unnaturally, did their best to discredit the new government by labelling it a Japanese creation. The Indonesians vigorously denied this and emphasized their republic's democratic ideals. The rest of the world, busy with the countless other problems created by the ending of the war, quite understandably paid little attention to the newly founded state. Meanwhile, as Allied troops began to replace the Japanese on the islands, conflicts broke out between Indonesian and European forces. By the middle of October the situation had become quite serious; but still there was little excitement outside Holland.

The Soviet Union, too, took no immediate stand. The first report on Indonesia to appear in *Pravda* after the independence declaration came on September 12, 1945. It discussed the English occupation of Timor, which island, it noted, was half Portuguese and half Dutch: no mention of an Indonesian Republic. On October 24 came the first statement in which the new government was noticed: *Pravda* reported that fighting in the "Dutch East Indies" was taking place between Netherlands troops and forces of The Indonesian government formed here under the leadership of Dr. Soekarno (sic(."

More reports concerning battles between the Indonesians and Allied troops followed; the country was now referred to as Indonesia rather than as the Dutch East Indies. On November 4 came the first critical comment: *Pravda* asked why the English, Americans, and Dutch, having declared that their countries stood for peace and universal human rights, saw fit to support colonial wars against the Vietnamese and Indonesian peoples. The United States, *Pravda* noted, took no further action against Dutch and British use of US lend-lease weapons than to request that the US labels be taken off the guns. By now, evidently, the USSR had decided to adopt a less-than-neutral stand on the issue, though Soviet comment had not gone so far as to take the part of the Sukarno government directly.

It was not until December 3 when, quoting a Reuters dispatch, the Soviet paper indirectly recognized the Republic's claim to legitimacy by referring to Republican premier Sjahrir as the "Prime Minister of Indonesia." From this time on, the Republic's government was consistently denoted as the rightful government of Indonesia, while the Netherlands Indies regime was considered merely as an arm of the Dutch occupation effort,[2] In the frequent short reports on Indonesia which appeared during the last two months of 1945, Russian comment was mostly restricted to facts concerning military operations and the spreading of the revolt; it was critical of the Dutch and British actions and of the American "hands-off" attitude, but did not go beyond what might be described as a liberally anti-colonial point of view.

It is interesting to note that the Soviet stand was considerably more cautious on the Indonesian question than was that of either the Dutch or the Australian Communist parties. The Australian party, doubtless influenced in part by those Indonesian Communists who had spent the war in that country, had taken a strong position behind Sukarno's Republic by early October; the Dutch Communists placed themselves fully behind the Indonesians a few weeks after this, as the fighting between British and Indonesian forces grew more serious. The Soviet Union was, of course, much less immediately concerned with the Indonesian situation than the Communists in either of these other countries; but it might also be noted that there were other important considerations making for a

---

[2]   It might further be noted in connection with the early Soviet attitude towards the Republic that Sukarno had sent a telegram to Stalin on the 1945 anniversary of the October Revolution, reportedly eliciting a response by Radio Moscow which declared:
"Allah grant that all the noble aims of the Indonesian people be successfully achieved." (Radio Moscow broadcast in Indonesian on November 15, 1945: as reported in *Merdeka*, November 16, 1945). Sukarno's message had read in part: "In the name of the Republic of Indonesia I congratulate you and the entire Russian people on the anniversary of the most important event in Russian history... We are convinced that Russia, which had striven for justice, freedom, and humanity, will, having become one of the four greatest powers, continue to remain true to its ideals." (Merdeka, November 12, 1945).

cautious stand on the Soviet side. Russia's wartime allies in Europe were the major imperial powers: to enter the lists against them on the colonial question would nave been a significant step towards the ending of the Alliance. The Soviet leaders, even if they were already convinced that the Allied cooperation would not long survive the war, may well have hesitated for other reasons to bring up the colonial problem at this time. In East Europe they had an enormous new sphere of influence which they desired to consolidate and have recognized by the other powers; in West Europe there was hope of Communist electoral victory, especially in colony-owning France. It is therefore perhaps not so strange that in the autumn of 1945 the Soviet Union did not choose to add the colonial issue to the agenda of its debate with the West.

In the few times that the colonial question was discussed in the early postwar period, Soviet comment seems to have been strongly influenced both by the relatively gradual approach of the Popular Front and by a sense of the tremendous revolutionary changes that had been brought about by World War II. There is a fluidity about Soviet analysis of the world situation in these days which is in striking contrast to the doctrinaire approach of the Comintern or the fierce partisanship which was to come a year or two later under the two camp doctrine.

In the wartime and early postwar periods the leading political-economic theorist in the Soviet Union was Eugene Varga, known best as the proponent of a relatively moderate stand in dealing with the West. Varga, impressed by the weakening of West European power during World War II, analyzed the colonial situation in a manner extraordinary for a Communist. He declared his belief that *"A completely new fact, without precedent in the history of imperialism, is the almost universal lessening of the financial dependence of the colonies and dependent countries on the empire, converting some colonies from the debtors to the creditors of the imperialist metropolis.* This course or development, which has been almost impossible to stop since the war, bears witness to far-reaching changes in the relationships between the colonies and the metropolis."[3]

Since Soviet Marxism had heretofore been accustomed to view the colonial scene as devoid of any hope for release from imperialist bondage

[3]   E. Varga, *Izmeneniia v ekonomike kapitalizma v itoge vtoroi mirovoi voini* (Gospolitizdat, 1946), p. 219. Author's emphasis. (Hereafter cited as *Izmeneniia*.)

short of revolution, this claim is remarkable indeed; for if the economic grip of the colonial power could be so loosened, then, in Marxist reasoning, its political hold would also weaken. Varga did qualify his statement a few pages later, though without denying its most important implication. "With the ending of the war, this process is clearly coming to a halt," he explained. "It is evident that within a few years after the war — with the appearance of the expected agrarian crisis — the indebtedness of the colonies and agrarian countries to other countries and especially to the United States will once again rise. However, the economic dependence of the majority of the colonies on their metropolis will never again be as strong as before the war."[4]

As to the political situation in the colonies, Varga noted that the war had given rise to tremendous political changes even in those countries which had not undergone Japanese occupation. There was a new upsurge in the anti-imperialist movement in the colonies, a new sharpening of the Asian crisis. The following factors had brought this about:

a) the economic development of the colonies strengthened the native bourgeoisie and the native proletariat — exactly those classes which generally take a leading position in the struggle for independence;

b) both warring camps made wide use in the war of native armed forces, which heightened the self-confidence of the colonial peoples;

c) the defeat by the Japanese of the former rulers (English, American, French) shattered the belief of the colonial peoples in the durability of white rule;

d) the war made it possible for a large number of natives to obtain weapons.[5]

---

[4]   Varga, *Izmeneniia*, p. 223.

[5]   Varga, *Izmeneniia*, p. 224. A comparison of this listing with one made in 1953 by Varga is interesting as an illustration of the increasing emphasis on the role of the proletariat and the Soviet Union which was to take place after 1947. In his later analysis Varga declared the factors behind the postwar rise in anti-imperialism to have been:

1. the victory of the Soviet Union — the fighter for the liberation of the peoples from the imperialist yoke — over the three mighty imperialist powers Japan, Germany, and Italy.

2. the development of industry and the development of an industrial proletariat, which took place in the war period in a number of colonies.

3. the defeat in the course of the second world war of the older colonial powers...by Japan;...

The most interesting point in this list of factors is Varga's reference to the bourgeoisie along with the proletariat as a leading element in the colonial revolution. This is an analysis on the lines of the "united front from above" policy, as we have seen it in our brief review of Communist policy before 1928. Coupled with the theory that the colonial countries were after the war economically less dependent on the metropolis, it made easy the acceptance and support of a bourgeois nationalist movement as the vehicle of a colonial revolution. In Varga's theory, then, there was no reason for the Soviet Union or the Indonesian Communists to oppose the Republic.

In addition to the internal pressure of a rising anti-imperialist movement, Varga saw the external force of United States policy applied against the colonial regimes. The US, he maintained, supported independence for the colonies because it hoped to gain from them the free hand for the economic penetration it had already obtained in South America and China.[6] Faced with such opposition from within and without, the colonial powers would be forced to make concessions, though giving them as little real content as possible. "The colonial powers," he argued, "will be forced to come towards the demands of the colonial population. New, transitional forms of colonial oppression will arise, with a final transformation to formally complete political independence with the preservation of economic dependence."[7]

This seemed to apply, however, only to the smaller dependent areas, such as Trans-Jordan.[8] To the greater dependencies, larger concessions would have to be made: "In relation to the more powerful colonies, especially India, the English bourgeoisie will be forced to make considerable concessions, up to the granting of dominion status."[9] Varga does not immediately explain just how much real independence this enhanced position would contain, but later he declares that "China and India, two countries whose populations compose about half the population of the

---

4. the mass arming of the colonial peoples during the war. .
5. the presence at the end of the war of a large amount of weapons in the hands of the colonial peoples, which made possible the creation of regular revolutionary armies." (Varga, *Osnovie voprosi ekonomiki i politiki imperializma (posle vtoroi mirovoi voini)*, (Akademiia Nauk SSSR, Institut ekonomiki; Gospolitizdat, 1953), p. 293.)
6. Varga, *Izmeneniia*, p. 225.
7. Varga, *Izmeneniia*, p. 318.
8. Varga, *Izmeneniia*, p. 226,
9. Varga, *Izmeneniia*, p. 226.

globe, can under certain circumstances carve out for themselves the position of world powers."[10]

This statement, along with Varga's previously cited opinion on the relative economic independence of the colonial countries in the postwar period, has considerable importance when connected with the impending transfer of sovereignty over India, Pakistan, Burma, and Ceylon by the British. Since previous Soviet doctrine on the colonial question had maintained that no peaceful weakening of the imperialist economic and political grip was possible, the independence of these countries could only be looked on as a farce and the new governments rejected as puppets of the imperialist power. Varga's view, however, gave a doctrinal opening for a more favorable attitude towards the ex-colonies' independence and thus towards the new Asian governments. To be sure, Varga did not go so far as to draw openly the conclusions that were latent in his theory; it may be he felt this would be climbing too far out on a political limb for comfort. Nonetheless, his statement that India could become a world power certainly indicates a feeling that that country's coming independence could have more than formal significance.

Towards the end of 1945, the colonial question was raised by the chief Soviet journal on foreign affairs. In this discussion revolutionary movements in Indonesia and Indochina were awarded considerable praise. However, it was declared that: "The defeat of Japanese imperialism, which tried in vain to create an enormous colonial empire in Asia, served as a signal to the exploited peoples of Southeast Asia to bring forward their just demands — for the guaranteeing of elementary democratic rights, for the securing of the opportunity for free political and economic development."[11] Not a word about sovereignty or immediate independence: the demands voiced here are still those of the popular front and the wartime alliance. The author warns — with apparent reference to Indonesia and Viet Nam — that a mere declaration of independence does not bring actual sovereignty; only freedom from the economic control of

---

[10] Varga, *Izmeneniia*, p. 318, It might be noted here that the China referred to in Varga's work is always Nationalist China, considered a semi-colonial country in the Soviet view.

[11] E. M. Zhukov, "Porazhenie iaponskogo imperializma i national'no- osvoboditel'naia bor'ba narodov Vostochnoi Azii," *Mirovoe khoziaistvo i mirovaia politika*, (No. 23(24, Nov.(Dec. 1945), p. 86. Zhukov, probably the leading authority on Far Eastern politics in the USSR Academy of Sciences, has frequently been given the task of formulating the doctrinal interpretation of Soviet Far Eastern policy.

the metropolis will guarantee this. Can such liberation be achieved only through revolution? Not necessarily, apparently; for the author points to UN trusteeship as a possible alternative to colonial domination:

The Charter of the United Nations envisages concrete possibilities for the progressive development of the colonial countries under the direction of an international organization. This direction, realized in the form of trusteeships, is to give the essential guarantees for the gradual development of the territories under trusteeship, "to promote the political, economic, social and educational advancement," to promote "the progressive development" of the population "towards self-government or independence."

This formula, clearly insufficient, was justly subjected to criticism at the San Francisco conference. All the same, trusteeship is capable of speeding up the progressive development of the colonies on the road to complete independence and is in any event able to secure the granting of elementary rights to the local population. Trusteeship does envisage control on the part of the UN, and, in particular, the presence in the Trusteeship Council of representations of UN members which do not participate immediately in the governing of trustee territories as well as those which do. The international character of trusteeship is aimed to a large degree at paralyzing the selfish tendencies which could be manifested by certain colonial circles should they desire to rule one or the other trustee territory "in the old-fashioned way."[12]

If this was representative of the Soviet attitude, there is little wonder that the European Communist parties did not take a stronger stand on the colonial issue. Neither the British, French, nor Dutch Communists asked for immediate independence for their country's colonial possessions in the autumn of 1945. Within the colonies, the gradualist slogans of the wartime period also remained: cooperation with the nationalists on the basis of a united front from above was advocated for the colonial Communist parties, and a moderate attitude on the independence issue was stressed. "Our Party," declared the Indian Communists, "is entering the electoral contest not to fight one or both of the Congress or the

---

[12] Zhukov, *Porazhenie*, p. 87. In connection with this, it might be noted that the Soviet Union was then engaged in an effort to secure four-power trusteeship over Korea, a project which may have influenced the USSR's attitude in this aspect of the Indonesian question. Cf. Max Beloff, *Soviet Policy in the Far East*, (London, 1953) pp. 159-163.

League, but to stand in the middle and fight the flame they both light by ourselves putting forward a plan of Indian freedom that embodies their just demands, but repudiates the unjust claims of both...”[13]

The Indonesian party, which had been re-established in October 1945 after a period of illegality lasting since the Communist-sponsored uprisings of 1927, took a less cooperative view. Under the leadership of the previously unknown Mohammad Jusuf, its insistence on uncompromising demands for immediate independence and its rejection of the republican government's relatively moderate foreign policy brought it by early 1946 into sharp contrast with the Communist line abroad and into conflict with the Indonesian government at home. It is thus not surprising that when former party leaders returned from wartime exile in Australia and the Netherlands, they undertook a purge of Jusuf's followers and laid down a policy of cooperation with the government and support of the negotiations with the Dutch.[14]

---

[13] “For a Free and Happy India,” *World News and Views*, (XXV, 47), December 1, 1945, p. 391. Quoted in Kautsky, *Moscow and the Communist Party of India*, p. 42.

[14] The new line for the Indonesian Communist Party (PKI) was established at a party conference begun on April 30, 1946, in Surakarta. For an account of the conference, cf. *Merdeka* (the major Indonesian nationalist newspaper of the time), May 3, 1946; and *Indonesia* (publication of the Perhimpunan Indonesia), XVI, 49 (June 1, 1946), p. 3. The manifesto issued by the conference, laying down the new line, is published in the aforementioned issue of *Indonesia* and in Merdeka of May 11, 1946.

At this conference Sardjono became chairman of the PKI; a pre-war Communist leader, he had been long resident in the concentration camp at Boven Digul, New Guinea, when World War II broke out. With the approach of the Japanese, the Dutch removed the inmates of Boven Digul to Australia; and Sardjono, along with other Indonesian Communists, worked for the Netherlands Indies government-in-exile during the war. In March, 1946, he was repatriated to the Indonesian Republic. Other Leftist leaders — notably Maruto Darusman, Setiadjit, and Abdulmadjid — had been pre-war leaders of the Perhimpunan Indonesia, an Indonesian student group in the Netherlands whose policies at that time were closely coordinated with those of the Dutch Communist Party. They worked in the anti-German underground during the war, and were repatriated to the Republic on April 29, 1946; the Dutch government was helpful in securing their return, apparently in the hope that their moderate opinions regarding relations between Indonesia and the Netherlands would have a favorable effect on the Republic's attitude in this matter.

In August Alimin, a prominent PKI leader who had fled abroad after the Communist uprisings of 1926-27, returned to share the leadership of the party with Sardjono. According to Alimin, he had lived in the Soviet Union until 1940, at which time he started back to Indonesia by way of China. He arrived in Yenan, but was forced by the blockade around the Chinese Communist forces there and the subsequent Japanese occupation of Indonesia to wait until the end of the war. At the beginning of 1946 he went to Hanoi by way of Chungking and Kunming; there he met Ho Chi Minh, After two weeks in Viet Nam he crossed the Mekong to Bangkok; from there he went to Malays, where he remained from the spring of 1946 until his return to Indonesia in August. Cf. Alimin, *Sepatah kata dari djaoeh*, (Djokjakarta, 1947), pp. 2-5.

1946-47: APPROBATION

The Soviet attitude towards the Indonesian situation might have continued to develop slowly in the pages of the Russian press had not circumstances in the United Nations at the beginning of 1946 led the USSR to come squarely to grips with the Western powers on the matter. Since the end of the war there had been a great deal of argument among the great powers over the continued military occupation of various smaller countries, the Soviet Union opposing British actions in Greece and the Near East, and Britain objecting strongly to the continued Soviet occupation of northern Iran. The Iranian question was brought up in the UN Security Council at its first session in London. The Soviet Union responded by introducing the matter of British military presence in Greece, Syria, Lebanon, and Indonesia. Two days after the Iranian problem was taken up by the UN, the Ukrainian delegate, Manuilsky, proposed that the Council look into the threat to world security presented by the Indonesian situation. This was on January 21; on February 7 the matter was brought up for debate. Manuilsky argued that the problem could hardly be considered an internal affair of the Netherlands, since it involved British and Japanese troops fighting against the Indonesian people. He suggested that the United Nations send an investigating commission to Indonesia. This suggestion was promptly turned down, with only Russia and Poland supporting the Ukraine on the measure. The Russian delegate, Andrei Vishinsky, then submitted an amendment to an Egyptian proposal for the withdrawal of English troops immediately after the disarmament of the Japanese in Indonesia; he asked that the Council recommend the setting up of a committee of investigation composed of the United States, (Nationalist) China, the USSR, and the Netherlands. This was rejected, only Russia, Poland, and Mexico supporting it; and the Egyptian resolution was likewise defeated. Meanwhile, the Indonesians themselves had resolved to try and bring the matter before the UN, an intention concerning which the USSR declared its hearty approval.[1]

Two points in these debates are worth our special attention. One is the evident Soviet preference for UN handling of the problem. No doubt one of the factors in this was, as we have previously noted, a desire to embarrass the British and counter their move on the Iranian question. If we keep in mind the Zhukov article of a few months before, however, it would seem that there might be more than this immediate tactical reason behind Soviet emphasis on the UN. We might even speculate whether the Russians did not quite realize in these early days how very circumscribed their UN role would become with the alliance of the great majority of countries against the Eastern bloc. If they were not so sanguine as to hope for some real say in trusteeship affairs, however, they seemed at least to realize by this point that they could gain excellent publicity in the Asian countries by championing the colonial cause in the UN. This propaganda opportunity gained added point with the development of Soviet-American enmity, when the USSR found it could use US hesitancy on the colonial issue as support for its allegation that American anti-colonialism was only a myth.

The situation was well illustrated in the ensuing development of the Indonesian issue, when the Soviet Union was able to gain considerable advantage from its support of the Republic in the Security Council. It is thus understandable that the USSR steadfastly supported UN jurisdiction over the Indonesian question so long as the UN body handling the matter contained a representative of the Soviet bloc. When, however, the problem was shunted off to a UN commission which contained no East European representatives, the Russians objected violently and concentrated their efforts on getting jurisdiction over the matter returned to the Security Council. The United States was not unaware of the situation either; and much of its efforts to mediate between the Indonesians and the Dutch arose from a desire to keep the question out of the Security Council.[2]

The second point of interest in the UN debate is that neither the Ukrainian nor the Soviet representative referred to an Indonesian government or claimed that the Republic was an independent state.

---

[1] Cf. "International Life," *New Times*, March 1, 1946, p. 15.

[2] Cf. Paul Kattenburg, "Indonesia," *The State of Asia* (ed. Lawrence K. Rossinger; New York, 1951), p. 418.

Rather, they talked of a "popular movement," whose desires they urged the colonial powers to consider. Since Soviet comment outside the UN was by this time freely referring to an Indonesian government, it would seem possible that the USSR may have hoped by its moderation to reduce Western objections to UN handling of the Indonesian question. If this thought was indeed entertained, it was quickly dashed by the imperial powers, who proved exceedingly sensitive to any attempts at bringing their colonial affairs under international control, especially an international control in which Soviet Russia participated. In the end, the Russians had to content themselves with the thought that their action on the Indonesian question had provided an embarrassing answer to the Iranian issue, and they made the most propagandistically of the matter:

The declarations of the representative of the Soviet Union disclosed to the entire world the way things really were. Greece, Indonesia, Syria and Lebanon have in fact been deprived of their national independence. This is the result of the illegal presence of foreign armed forces — English force, and in Syria and Lebanon also French. The results of the discussion of the questions of Greece, Indonesia, Syria and Lebanon in the Security Council demonstrated with crystal clarity that the policy defended by Mr. Bevin is of a distinctly anti-democratic character.[3]

Soviet relations with Great Britain, never very cordial even during the wartime alliance, reached a low point in the year just after the war, before the US-Soviet quarrel had really gained momentum. Russian comment at this time pictured Britain as the worst of the imperialist powers. This line was reflected in Soviet discussion of Indonesia, which country British troops were occupying in preparation for the return of the Dutch. The English, it was claimed, were not pulling the Dutch chestnuts out of the nationalist fire for nothing; Britain hoped that by preserving Dutch rule it could prevent English economic interests in Indonesia from being displaced by American capital:

After the Second World War, when the USA became economically and financially the most powerful of all the capitalist countries, interested English circles were particularly concerned for the conditions under which their economic activity in the countries of Southeast Asia would develop in the postwar period. It was evident to them that only the

---

[3] *Pravda*, February 24, 1946.

consolidation of Dutch sovereignty could serve in any measure to secure the position of English capital in Indonesia. Another and not less important consideration, which was closely connected not only with Indonesia but with the colonies of England itself, also dictated the necessity of full English support of Holland. The events in Indonesia were taking place directly at the threshold of British colonies — Malaya, Burma, and India. The liberation of Indonesia could have seemed to them a too dangerous and contagious example.[4]

"On the other hand," it was declared, "it seemed that suitable possibilities for and even the actual achievement of political independence by Indonesia could be extremely beneficial to the economy of the USA, which did not need to fear, as did the other colonial powers, the 'infectious' consequences of independence in Indonesia. From the point of view of securing the necessary conditions for the unlimited penetration of American capital and for more advantageous opportunities for competition with capital of other countries, the broadest possible autonomy for Indonesia and even its separation from the metropolis were of no little interest to the USA."[5] It is apparent from such comment that the Soviet analysts expected fairly strong US backing for the colonial independence movements. When the United States proved considerably more hesitant in supporting nationalism, this theory had to be rectified, as we shall presently see.

Commenting on the internal situation in Indonesia, the Soviet Union strongly advocated a broad united front from above, "The distinguishing tendencies of this movement, which is developing rapidly but unevenly in all colonial countries," it was declared of the national-liberation movement, "are, first, a definite tendency towards the unification of the most varied levels of the population and of the classes of these countries for the achievement of a single, all-national task; and, secondly, the ever-increasing weight of the masses in this movement. It is exactly these conditions which give the present process in the colonial countries a special

---

[4]   A. A. Guber, *Natsional'no-osvoboditel'noe dvizhenie v Indonezii*, (Moscow, 1946), p. 12. Public lecture delivered on March 27, 1946, in the Moscow Lecture Hall. Professor Guber, the present head of the USSR Academy of Sciences' Pacific Institute, is the leading Soviet authority on Indonesia. For other Soviet comments on the role of Great Britain in the Indonesian question, see V. Vasil'eva, "Sobitiia v Indonezii," *Mirovoe khoziaistvo i mirovaia politika*, (No. 1(2), Jan.(Feb., 1946, p. 93; "International Life," *New Times*, August 15, 1946, p. 18; and I. Kopylov, "The Events in Indonesia," *New Times*, (No. 19), October 1, 1946.

[5]   Guber, *Natsional'no-osvoboditel'noe dvizhenie*, p. 18.

strength and significance."[6] Insofar as the anti-imperialist movement was not united, the Republic was criticized: "…it is an indubitable fact that the Indonesian liberation movement is subject to great internal difficulties as a result of the absence of a single, firm leadership. …In the leadership of the national movement there are, it is apparent, hesitant, less consequent elements as well as leftist groups. Sukarno himself has followed a career typical for a bourgeois nationalist."[7]

In spite of the doubt expressed here as to Sukarno's revolutionary steadfastness, the Soviet Union apparently considered that the united front should remain under the leadership of the bourgeois nationalist movement. To this end, very little emphasis was placed on the failings of the Indonesian leaders: the above comment is almost the only critical remark uttered before 1948. Moreover, the collaborationist past of some of the more prominent Indonesian nationalists was forgiven, a clemency the Soviet Union did not lightly accord. "This circumstance' it was considered, "was widely utilized by the Dutch from the very beginning to brand the entire movement led by Sukarno as one inspired by the Japanese";[8] and on the grounds that it served imperialist ends the charge was dismissed.

We may wonder why the Soviet Union chose to support the Indonesian nationalists instead of encouraging leadership of the revolution by the pro-Communist Left, which by 1947 had become powerful enough to replace Sjahrir as premier with the left socialist Amir Sjarifuddin. We cannot, of course, offer any certain answer to this question, but can perhaps make a few suggestions as to possibilities .

In the first place, it should be kept in mind that, until 1948 at least, the Soviet Union tended to advance the same strategy in Asia as it did in Europe; and in Europe it was concerned at this time with the development of a united front from above which would give the Communists a strong place within the existing governmental structure. It was in Europe, and not in Asia, that the brightest chances for Communist success were seen; and such statements as the following on Indochina are perhaps some

---

[6]   Guber, *Natsional'no-osvoboditel'noe dvizhenie*, p. 4.
[7]   Vasil'eva, *Sobitiia*, p. 91. Cf. also Guber, "The Situation in Indonesia," *New Times*, February 15, 1946, pp. 9-10; and O. Zabozlayeva, "Indonesia," *New Times*, April 15, 1946, p. 26 for comments urging a broad united front from above in Indonesia. In India, the same need for national unity was seen: cf. V. Bushevich, "Bor'ba Indii za nezavisimost'," *Mirovoe khoziaistvo i mirovaia politika*, (No. 9), Sept. 1946, p. 52.
[8]   Guber, *Natsional'no-osvoboditel'noe dvizhenie*, p. 10.

indication of how much the Asian situation was made an adjunct of developments in Europe: "The further growth of Viet Nam[9] depends to a considerable extent on its connections with a democratic France, whose progressive, democratic forces would consistently support the colonial liberation movement."[10]

Secondly, and no doubt of critical importance, was the advantage gained by the Soviet Union in the propaganda war through its stand as the champion of Asian nationalism in the UN. In view of the fact that the Indonesian question was dealt with by the Security Council several times in the course of the revolution, it is not difficult to see why the USSR might have considered it the wiser course to forget that the Indonesian leaders were not all that was desired.

Perhaps, too, the Russians were to a certain extent deceived by the rapid rise to prominence of the Indonesian left wing. The Sajap Kiri coalition of leftist parties formed during 1946 and 1947 the backbone of political support for the government's relatively conciliatory program vis-a-vis the Dutch. Sardjono, chairman of the PKI since his return from Australia in the spring of 1946, was appointed head of the National Concentration, an all-party grouping set up under government inspiration. Due to sharp political disunity, the organization existed almost solely on paper; but the Russians, who gave every indication of being ill-informed about the internal politics of the Republic, seemed unaware of this. Again, the representation of the leftist groupings in the KNIP (the Indonesian emergency parliament) was increased considerably by President Sukarno in the beginning of 1947, partly because of their growing popular support and partly because the government leaders saw in the Left Wing's more moderate nationalism a source of support for their negotiations with the Dutch. The Communist

Party benefitted particularly, its representation going from one seat to thirty-five.

By 1947, Soviet commentators apparently found the situation in Indonesia favorable enough to make such statements as the following:

The democratic elements in the country have become a major

---

9   Ho Chi Minh's Viet Nam. For the sake of uniformity and brevity, this paper follows Communist usage and refers to the Ho Chi Minh government as Viet Nam rather than Viet Minh.

10   V. Vasil'eva, "Viet Nam — indokitaiskaia demokraticheskaia respublika," *Mirovoe khoziaistvo i mirovaia politika*, (No. 12), Dec. 1946, p. 89.

force. The Communist Party of Indonesia...is one of the largest and most influential parties in the Indonesian Republic. Although only one representative of the Communist Party is participating in the Sjarifuddin government, its influence in the country is great. The Communist Party heads the National Concentration, an organization which unites all Indonesian political parties. The Communist Party is now numerically the largest party in Indonesia.[11]

Such an optimistic assertion may of course be ascribed in large part to propagandistic bluster. At the same time, however, it should be noted that the only other Asian countries about which the same attitude was expressed were China and Ho Chi Minh's Viet Nam, about which there was much better reason to consider that the Communists might be able to take control of the nationalist movement. In point of fact, Indonesia and Viet Nam were almost always cited together as if the two republics were of the same political nature. Viet Nam and Indonesia were leading a "true war of national liberation," it was declared;[12] and during 1946 and 1947 the two names were increasingly linked together in Soviet discussions of the colonial revolution.[13]

Could it be that, with their lack of information on the Indonesian situation, the Russians were misled into a gross over-estimation of pro-Communist strength in Indonesia? If the Soviets were deceived by the Marxist terminology and the revolutionary, anti-capitalist declarations of Indonesia's nationalist leaders, it would not have been the first time in history they were so taken in. We remember the Chinese revolution of the 1920's, when the revolutionary Marxist bearing of the Kuomintang's leaders helped lull the Russians into a belief that the nationalist leaders

---

[11] V. A. Avarin, *Politicheskie izmeneniia na tikhom okeane posle vtoroi mirovoi voini* (Moscow, 1947), p. 13.

[12] Avarin, *Politicheskie izmeneniia*, p. 11; cf. also Guber, *Natsional'no-osvoboditel'noe dvizhenie*, p. 4; E. M. Zhukov, "Velikaia Oktiabr'skaia sotsialisticheskaia revoliutsiia i kolonial'nii Vostok," *Bol'shevik*, (No. 20), October 1946, pp. 45-46.

[13] In evaluating the extent to which the Russians were overly sanguine in their hopes for the Indonesian situation it is, of course, of critical importance to know whether or not certain of the supposedly non-Communist leaders of the Sajap Kiri actually were secret members of the PKI at this time, as they claimed a year later. If it is true, the major Left Wing leaders, except for Sjahrir, were Communists; and from July 1947 to January 1948 Indonesia had a Communist premier (Amir Sjarifuddin). Opinions as to the truthfulness of their assertions have been many and strong; but unfortunately the writer has been unable to find anything that might be viewed as concrete proof one way or the other, and so we must leave this vital portion of the picture a blank.

were a good deal more sympathetic to the Communist cause than was actually the case. Then, too, there was the fact of the Left Wing's increasing power and the dependence of the government on its support: there was at least some good reason to hope that after the independence of the country had been assured the Communist-oriented political elements would be in a position to influence and perhaps take over the government. In this case, it might have seemed unwise for the extreme left to press its cause too far at this time: for if it failed, the non-Communist forces would be alienated and its chances of later assuming power would be seriously diminished; while if it won, the all-important American pressure against Dutch military intervention would very likely be removed. If this was indeed a Soviet consideration, then the survival of the Republic was the most important task for the Communists, at that time, and the interests of the nationalists and Communists would run parallel for the duration of the revolution.

It might be appropriate to interject here some observations on a dilemma which has always affected the Soviet attitude towards Communist movements in other countries. It has frequently been observed that the interests of Russian diplomacy are not always identical with those of international Communism, as was well evidenced during the pre-war period, when Soviet foreign policy and the activities of the Comintern were all too often a source of embarrassment to each other. That the Soviet Union tended to value its state interest above the welfare of the other Communist parties is reflected in the decline and eventual abandonment of the Comintern.

When dealing with the colonial question, the matter was even more complicated from the Soviet point of view. In the first place, as we have previously noted, the USSR was well aware of the fact that what went on in the colonies affected politics in the motherland, and it was careful not to push the colonial issue too strongly when it wanted to preserve good relations with the European power. Secondly, the Soviet Union showed, in actual practice, a distinct disbelief that the Communists could really lead the national revolution in a colonial or semi-colonial country. This may have been reflection of the general Soviet contempt for the abilities of the other Communist parties, a disdain which became increasingly evident as the years failed to produce another successful Communist revolution. It may also have had its origin in the experience of the Russian revolution, when Lenin had argued to such good effect that the first task of the Bolsheviks was to help the bourgeoisie gain power over the feudal regime, and that only after the bourgeois-democratic revolution had been accomplished were they to turn on their erstwhile allies and seize power from them. While this strategy was not made dogma for the Asian Communists, it may have encouraged Stalin's disastrous belief that the Communists could squeeze the Kuomintang like a lemon and then throw it away; and the same psychology may also have been of some weight in Soviet support of the Indonesian nationalists in the period discussed in this paper.

It is perhaps superfluous to point out that the "lessons of October," great as their prestige was in Soviet thought, were actually applicable only to a certain, rather unusual revolutionary situation. The Leninist analysis implied that only the bourgeoisie (in the colonial case, bourgeois nationalists) would be strong enough to lead the revolution against the feudal(colonial government; but once they achieved power they would not have the strength to maintain themselves or dispose of the Communists. On the other hand, the Communists would not be strong enough themselves to seize power from the feudal(colonial regime but would be able to take it from the bourgeois nationalists. In the case of the Russian revolution this was a perfectly valid assumption; but, as Chiang Kai-shek demonstrated in the 1920's, it was quite possible that the nationalists would not only be strong enough to lead the revolution but, having squeezed the Communists out like a lemon, to ungratefully throw them away.

Whatever feelings may have underlain the Soviet scepticism as to the prospects of Communist colonial victory, it had the practical effect of strengthening Soviet support for anti-Western nationalist movements in preference to emphasis on local Communist victory. This found perhaps its earliest — and crassest — expression in Russian support of Kemal's Turkey even after its bloody purge of the Turkish Left:

We know quite well that, for example, Communists are murdered in just as base a manner in Kemalist Turkey as in social-democratic bourgeois Germany. Naturally the CI *(the* Communist International) will battle most sharply against such methods of struggle and against the persecution of Communists in general. However, the CI will continue its support in cases where a really great revolutionary movement — perhaps half-nationalist, but really revolutionary — is in process, insofar as this movement is directed against all imperialism;…[14]

What all this comes down to is that the Soviet Union was willing to support a government, non-Communist or even anti-Communist, as long as the foreign policy of that government was in line with that of the Soviet Union We see this carried over into the postwar period, when the Soviet Union backed the Indonesian Republic, which was at odds with the Dutch, and exhibited grave doubts about the Indian nationalists, who were coming to an agreement with the British, although the leaders of both Asian groups held approximately the same views regarding Communism.

So far we have made very little mention of China in our discussion of the Soviet attitude on Asia in this period, though that country was a busy center of Communist activity and Soviet interest. In point of fact, however, there was surprisingly little mention of the Chinese Communists and of the Chinese civil war in Soviet comment during 1946 and 1947. Sometimes the Chinese conflict was ranked alongside the Vietnamese and Indonesian struggle and sometimes not; certainly there was no general recognition of the Chinese Communists' distinctive views or consideration that they formed the example for Asia. On the contrary, the patterns for the Asian revolution appeared, if anything, to be Viet Nam and Indonesia, which were "carrying high the banner of freedom, the banner of struggle for independence, into the very heart of Asia."[15] It seems fairly evident that until surprisingly late in the game the Soviet Union was doubtful of Communist success in the Chinese civil war. This attitude, which constitutes a striking disbelief in the prospects of immediate Communist victory in Asia, was reflected in the USSR's reluctance to support the Chinese Communists after World War II and its continued recognition of the Kuomintang government as the legal government of China.[16] It is doubtful if the Chinese Communists would have been so thoroughly abandoned had the Russians realized that they

---

[14] Zinoviev, at the third Comintern congress (1921). *Protokolle des III. Kongresses der Kommunistischen Internationale,* (Hamburg, 1921), p. 1010.

[15] E. M. Zhukov, "K polozheniu v Indii," *Mirovoe khoziaistvo i mirovaia politika,* (No. 7), July, 1947, p. 3.

[16] It has also been pointed out that another reason for the Soviet effort to maintain good relations with the Nationalist government may have been a desire to prevent further American intervention in the Chinese civil war: cf. Max Beloff, *Soviet Policy in the Far East* (London, 1953), p. 43. Beloff shares the opinion that the Soviet Union at this time apparently did not believe the Chinese Communists could gain power by themselves (Ibid., p. 36).

were very soon to become the masters of China; but all outward indications are that the USSR still felt this an unlikely prospect.

It would, of course, be highly desirable to find some link between Soviet comment and actual events in Indonesia, to check whether, as in the case of China, Russian actions would correspond to the attitude apparent in Soviet writings. There is such a link: but unfortunately, as we shall see, it by no means constitutes a water-tight proof.

Both Soviet comment and Indonesian Communist policy emphasized the necessity of supporting the nationalist movement and preserving the unity of Indonesian anti-imperialist forces during this period. The Soviet press looked with considerable sympathy on the moderate socialist premier Sjahrir right up to the time of his fall in June 1947,[17] giving him probably more favorable coverage than any other Indonesian leader up to that time. In that month, however, Sjahrir found it necessary to make considerable concessions to the Dutch in the face of a Netherlands ultimatum. The more radical Left Wing leaders — Tan Ling Djie, Abdulmadjid, Wikana, Amir Sjarifuddin — refused to sanction these concessions and by withdrawing their support from Sjahrir brought about his resignation. On the same day that these events took place, Setiadjit, a prominent Left Wing leader, returned from Europe, where he had been attending a conference of the Communist-oriented World Federation of Trade Unions in Prague. He immediately met with the other Sajap Kiri leaders, and in an excellent speech he gave an exposition of his experiences of the W.F.T.U. conference in Prague and the general situation in Europe-1947, thus stressing to them that Mr Sjahrir's view on the Indonesian issues and the relations of the big powers with regard to it, is just! We may safely assume that Mr. Setiadjid's argumentation has evidently caused the sudden change of view of the Left Wing,..."[18] The Sajap Kiri leaders, on hearing Setiadjit, reversed their position and asked Sjahrir to return to office. Sjahrir did not resume his post; but when Sjarifuddin took up the job in his stead he proved willing to grant even more concessions to the Dutch than Sjahrir had.

It seems fairly safe to assume that Setiadjit, who was important but by no means the final authority in the Left Wing grouping, was backed by more than his own personal opinion if he was to cause such a complete

---

[17] Cf., for example articles in *Izvestia*, June 4, 1947; and *Trud*, June 13, 1947.

[18] *The Voice of Free Indonesia*, June 1947, p. 548, (An Indonesian government publication (.

shift on the part of the other Sajap Kiri leaders. He, Sjarifuddin, Wikana, Tan Ling Djie, and Abdulmadjid all claimed a year later to have been secret members of the Communist Party at this time;[19] if we accept their claim the question of "orders from Moscow" naturally arises in the matter of the June reversals. It must be noted that there is no definite proof of these leaders' actually having been party members before 1948; but all of them were far from unsympathetic to Communism in the period at hand and would doubtless have given considerable weight to European Communist opinion. Here, however, we face the problem of not knowing in how far Setiadjit, if he had tried to transmit the European Communist view, was rendering an accurate interpretation of it, for the specific events to which his actions were related (though only Sjahrir's fall, not the Dutch ultimatum or his reaction to it) occurred only after Setiadjit had left Europe, and so he could have received no direct reaction to them. Again, we might note that Setiadjit spent some time in the Netherlands on his trip; and the possibility should not be excluded that he there came to appreciate the Dutch intention to attack at the slightest provocation. It may be that the radical Left Wing leaders had not previously been aware of the extreme gravity of the situation and that they reversed their position and made further concessions in the hopes of staving off a Dutch attack. Lastly, we cannot be sure that Setiadjit, if he was influenced by European Communist opinion, was not transmitting the Dutch Communist view rather than the Soviet attitude. In view of our present inability to answer these important questions, therefore, we cannot point to the Sajap Kiri's reversal as tangible evidence of Soviet policy in Indonesia.[20]

---

[19]   Cf. George McT. Kahin, *Nationalism and Revolution in Indonesia* (Ithaca, 1953), p. 273.

[20]   It should be noted that some later criticism of the Sjahrir concessions was voiced on the Soviet part, the following version of the cabinet's fall being given:

Notwithstanding the fully understandable indignation of the Indonesian people at the aggressive policy of Holland, the Republican government of Sutan Sjahrir took a conciliatory position. It still hoped to avoid the outbreak of a bloody war. Indignation at the Dutch ultimatum was shown in the Indonesian parliament and in the political parties whose leaders had entered into the Sjahrir government.

A resolution sharply criticizing the conciliatory position of the Sjahrir cabinet was introduced into the Indonesian cabinet.

Late in the evening of the same day, June 26, Sjahrir handed President Sukarno the cabinet's resignation...

After a stormy debate in parliament, the resolution against the Sjahrir cabinet was taken back. However, the cabinet was not able to renew its work in its former composition.

(A. Guber, *Voina v Indonezii* (Moscow, 1947), p. 16. Public lecture delivered August 7, 1947, in the

In considering the Russian position, it should be kept in mind that Soviet comment on the Indonesian situation never openly urged compromise on the part of the Indonesians; and indeed it was patently not in the interests of the USSR to play the role of discourager of the Indonesian revolution. What support it lent to the moderate view was of a passive sort, consisting mostly of praise for the moderate Republican leaders, especially Sjahrir. Similarly, the Soviet press voiced no objections to the Indonesians' conclusion of the Linggadjati Agreement with the Netherlands at the end of 1946, except for some well-founded doubts as to whether the Dutch intended to keep the truce it entailed.

The July "police action" by the Netherlands against the Republic led to a sharp Soviet denunciation of the Dutch and a condemnation of Netherlands perfidy in breaking its agreement with the Indonesians. "All this bears witness to the fact that the Linggadjati Agreement was for the Dutch forces only a manoeuvre taken to gain time," *Izvestia* declared. As for the reason behind the attack, the paper contended that "It need only be remembered that up to this time Dutch interests have been selling Indonesian 'futures' to the American monopolists, who are covetous of the rubber, tin, oil and other riches of Indonesia. Having received such solid support, the Dutch colonizers went over into open military action against the Indonesian people,"[21]

Note that in this analysis American imperialists have replaced the British as the power supporting the Dutch. This change, which had been developing since the latter part of 1946, can be explained specifically in the Indonesian case by the fact that by late 1946 the British troops had left Indonesia. However, the substitution of the American imperialist menace for the British was a general phenomenon in Soviet comment on the colonial question at this time, and it seems quite safe to label it a product of the gathering cold war between the Soviet Union and the United States.

Moscow Lecture Hall.)
Since, however, this analysis was made after the failure of the Sjahrir and Sjarifuddin concessions to prevent the Dutch from attacking, the likelihood is too great that it is an *ex post facto* criticism for us to accept it as evidence of the original Soviet attitude to the concessions; and, unfortunately, the writer has so far found no Soviet opinion on the matter expressed before the Dutch attack.
[21] *Izvestia*, July 25, 1947, Cf. also articles in the *Izvestia* issues of August 1 and 27, 1947; O. Chechetkina, "In Indonesia," *New Times*, July 20, 1947, pp. 18-24; and "The War in Indonesia," *New Times*, July 20, 1947, pp. 1-2, for reactions to the Dutch attack.

Since America had shown much less inclination to take sides with the colonies against their European masters than Soviet analysis had originally prophesied, the Communists also began to revise their theories on the American attitude towards the colonial situation. The United States was afraid to go all the way in supporting the independence movement, it was considered: for the American imperialists feared the colonial masses, once freed of foreign domination, would not allow themselves to be exploited by American interests. Therefore, the analysis ran, the United States sought to work through the colonial powers in cases where the nationalist movement seemed too independent for American tastes. Thus, it was alleged, the United States stood behind the Dutch in their police action and tried to keep the Security Council out of the picture:

…the government of the USA has done everything in order that, in the first place, the UN might be kept from handling the Indonesian question, and, secondly, to demonstrate to the Dutch government that it could wholly rely on American cooperation in its war against the Indonesian Republic.

The "good offices" (offered by the US to both sides after the Dutch attack), which the American officials bedeck with talk about the defense of independence and the democratic rights of the people, serve to encourage the Dutch colonizers in their efforts to put down the liberation movement in Indonesia. Former Indonesian premier Sjahrir was perfectly justified in stating at a press conference in Washington that "the American position in relation to the independence won by the Indonesians has been deeply disappointing."[22]

We have previously discussed the Soviet desire to keep the Indonesian question under the jurisdiction of the Security Council and the probable motives underlying it. However, when in August 1947 the Council voted to set up a Committee of Good Offices, with no East European representation, to observe the cease-fire arrangements in Indonesia, the Russians did not invoke their veto. No doubt a factor in this restraint was a realization on the Soviet side that to do so would mean that no action at all would be taken by the UN and that responsibility for this might be

---

[22] *Izvestia*, September 25, 1947

placed on the USSR.[23] No love was lost by the Russians on the committee, though, and for the rest of the revolution the Soviet Union made every effort to get the Indonesian problem back under the direct supervision of the Security Council, where the Eastern bloc could also make its voice heard.

---

[23] The Soviet Union took an exemplary stand in the UN discussions from the Indonesian point of view. It supported an Australian proposal calling for an immediate cease-fire and arbitration by a third party; this was defeated when the US threw its weight against it. The Russians called for the withdrawal of Dutch forces to pre-attack positions; only Poland voted for this. They then supported an American compromise proposal calling for a cease-fire. When Sjahrir arrived to plead the Indonesian case at the UN and called for a return to the original Australian proposal, with a return of Dutch troops to their prior positions, he was supported only by the USSR and Poland. A Soviet proposal to establish a commission of Security Council representatives to watch over the execution of the cease-fire order was supported by most Council members, including the US, but vetoed by France. The French, no doubt with the Indochina situation in mind, would only allow the commission to observe, not superintend, the cease-fire, and demanded that the commission consist of representatives of governments having career consuls at Batavia. This automatically excluded the East European members of the Council, Russia and Poland, plus two other pro-Indonesian countries, Colombia and Syria (Cf. Kahin, *Nationalism and Revolution*, p. 217, note 13), Finally, the Americans proposed a Committee of Good Offices, of which one member would be elected by each of the two sides and the third member by the two thus chosen. This proposal was finally accepted, over Russian, Polish, and Syrian abstention.

THE TWO CAMP DOCTRINE

So far, the Soviet attitude towards Southeast Asia had developed fairly gradually towards a firmer support of the revolutionary independence movement. In the fall of 1947, however, the Soviet world view underwent a drastic revision which was to have great significance for the Indonesian revolution. The change was not without portent, since for some time Soviet-Western relations had been growing rapidly worse, and it was obvious that the Popular Front tactics and the postwar attempts to win parliamentary power in West Europe were long outmoded. The widening gap between the two points of view left less and less room for any compromise or any neutralism.

In Asia those countries which, like Indonesia, were at daggers drawn with the colonial powers did not feel at first any adverse effects of this change; if anything, it was to their advantage, for it meant stronger Soviet opposition to the colonial powers. For India, Burma, and those other colonies which were finding a peaceful road to independence, the case was quite different. We remember Varga's theory that since World War II the colonial countries had been economically much less dependent on the metropolis. This analysis had given a doctrinal opportunity for deviation from the old Marxist argument that no imperial power would peacefully grant real independence to a colony, so that if the Soviet Union chose to adopt a favorable attitude towards the new Asian governments, here was its excuse. The Soviet Union, however, did not choose to do so. During 1946 and early 1947 Russian comment on the Indian question was hesitant, apparently not yet having determined on an attitude towards the new state and its leaders. In that time, the march of events elsewhere in the world made it less and less likely that the USSR would look with favor upon any nation which tried to straddle the gulf between East and West.

Gradually, Varga's theories lost their authority. In discussions of the colonial question, the optimistic view expressed by him on the colonies' economic position was replaced by arguments that the colonies had gained nothing, not even as a result of the war: "In the vast majority of the colonies there was not created, even as a result of the Second World War, the basic pre-requisites for their economic independence: they lack every industry, do not produce the means of production, do not have machines."[1] On this count, it was declared, the colonial powers could feel safe in allowing them formal independence and the development of some light industry; for the imperialists would remain in real control of the economy, and they would "calculate that, being the bosses of the colonies, they will be able to direct the process of their capitalist development and, at the proper moment, will be able to call a halt to this development, as they did after the First World War."[2]

Such a pessimistic view augered ill for Soviet sympathy towards Britain's former colonies. Other developments in Soviet colonial theory were also pointing to a less compromising view towards the Asian nationalists. In the spring of 1947, the Economics Institute of the Soviet Academy of Sciences held a session to discuss the Varga doctrine. As was to be expected, Varga's theories were vigorously condemned. On the colonial issue, however, no new dogma had apparently been decided on: and there took place one of those rare events in Stalinist Russia, a political argument. I. A. Shneerson, who presented the main denunciation of Varga, developed in his exposition the thesis that the development of two opposing political camps had affected the colonial situation by sharpening the conflict between the imperialist powers and the national-liberation movement; in Indonesia, Viet Nam, and China, he noted, it had come to open combat. On the other hand, such a considerable growth of working class strength has frightened the colonial grande bourgeoisie, so that it is willing to come to an agreement with any imperialism — English or American. The national bourgeoisie of a number of colonies has completely and irrevocably entered on the road of national betrayal. Hegemony in the national-liberation movement of the colonial peoples has in a number of colonies passed into the hands of the working class.

---

[1]   V. Vasil'eva, Noveishie tendentsii v politike imperialists," *Mirovoe khoziaistvo i mirovaia politika*, May 1947, p. 64.

[2]   Vasil'eva, *Noveishie tendentsii,* p. 64.

Together with this, conditions are being created for the realization of reforms of a socialist character alongside those of anti-feudal and anti-imperialist nature, conditions for a struggle of an original sort for a people's democracy."[3]

A number of the other delegates found themselves unable to accept the far-reaching implications of Shneerson's thought. The economist Lemin argued that "in a number of colonial countries a united popular front is still possible to a certain extent with progressive segments of the bourgeoisie."[4] China specialist Maslennikov shared this objection: "Naturally there exists in the colonial countries a radical, democratically inclined bourgeoisie, which must not be completely alienated from participation in the national-liberation movement." "However," he added, "its role must not be overestimated."[5]

At the bottom of this discussion lay a basic problem of Communist tactics in the colonial world. Communist policy in this area had, since the 1920's been formulated in terms of the role played by what came to be called the "national bourgeoisie" — an ill-defined group that included local entrepreneurs, civil servants, intellectuals, and so on. The national bourgeoisie was a class located, in the Communist analysis, somewhere between the petty bourgeoisie, which could be counted on to support the colonial revolution, and the compradore bourgeoisie, a segment of the grande bourgeoisie which identified its interests with those of the imperialists. The national bourgeoisie generally supported the independence movement, but it was unreliable since, if the working class movement became too strong within the revolutionary camp, it was likely to desert the national cause on the theory that the imperialists presented the lesser of two evils. Now all this sounds like an abstruse bit of Marxist dialectic until we realize that the Communists almost invariably identified the national bourgeoisie with the non-Communist nationalist movement, and that when it was decreed that the national bourgeoisie had gone over to the imperialist camp it meant the end of Communist cooperation with the nationalist movement. Thus it was decided in 1923 at the Sixth Comintern Congress that the national bourgeoisie had deserted

---

[3]   "Poslevoennoe obostrenie obshchevo krizisa kapitalisma," *Mirovoe khoziaistvo i mirovaia politika,* (No. 6), June 1947, p. 107. (Hereafter referred to as *Poslevoennoe obostrenie*).

[4]   *Poslevoennoe obostrenie,* p. 111.

[5]   *Poslevoennoe obostrenie,* p. 115.

the revolution, and Communist parties were instructed to oppose the nationalist movements as traitors to the revolution. It is this position towards which Shneerson leaned and towards which Maslennikov and Lemin were not yet willing to go. The function of the Soviet political scholar being less to develop his own analysis than to provide a doctrinal justification for the policies of the State, this breach in the monolithic unity of Stalinist political thought would seem a fair indication that the scholars concerned were as yet unaware of any clear-cut Soviet policy on the question at hand.

Reflecting the apparent fact that no decision had been reached regarding the colonial situation, the Soviet attitude towards India continued to show no clear line. The Nehru-inspired Inter-Asian Relations Conference was viewed by the Soviet as playing "a conspicuous, progressive role in the life of the Asian countries"; it was hoped the meeting would make for greater Asian solidarity against the imperialist menace.[6]

About the same time, however, E. M. Zhukov came forth with an analysis of Indian politics in which he abandoned all tolerance towards the Indian national bourgeoisie and declared that "the activity of the Indian working class, its leading role in the struggle against English rule, is pushing the grande bourgeoisie more and more strongly into the imperialist camp, causing it to take an anti-national position."[7] It is the grande bourgeoisie, he considered, that formed the backbone of Ghandism, which it saw as a philosophy that would dull the popular political conscience and lead it from the fight against the imperialists. Neutralism was no policy of true impartiality but was a tactic adopted by the bourgeoisie to justify its collaboration with British capitalism against American economic penetration of India: "...in Indian bourgeois circles there is a wide-spread 'theory' of the necessity of observing 'neutrality' in a conflict which might arise due to American expansion. In point of fact, this 'theory' of neutrality serves to justify a policy of

[6]   *Izvestia*, May 31, 1947.
[7]   E. M. Zhukov, "K polozheniiu v Indii," *Mirovoe khoziaistvo i mirovaia politika*, (No. 7), July 1947, p. 6 This version is not Zhukov's original report, which was delivered before the Academy of Social Sciences on May 11, 1947, but an abridgement of it made by Zhukov. We do not know, of course, whether the rapidly changing political situation at that time caused him to alter the emphasis of the report before publication. Not too much significance can therefore be attached to the exact date; and we should probably best consider it simply as coming from the late spring or early summer of 1947.

collaboration with English capitalism, a policy of establishing closer contact between the Indian bourgeoisie and English capital."[8] In the face of this discouraging picture, Zhukov expressed the now-familiar hope that the Indonesian and Vietnamese examples would not be without effect on India.[9]

In June, the USSR Academy of Sciences held a joint session of the Pacific Institute and the Institutes of History, Philosophy, Economics, Law, and Language and Literature to discuss the subject of India. In the political discussions, opinion was again divided on the role of the Indian national bourgeoisie, but the voices supporting the Indian nationalists were noticeably weak.

Soviet Indian specialist Mel'man presented the thesis that the Indian bourgeoisie had been considerably strengthened during the war due to the rapid development of Indian industry at that time. This class nursed a strong resentment against the English, who sought to prevent the increase of native capitalist competition. The grudge was forgotten, however, when the Indian masses showed signs of becoming too strong for bourgeois tastes. There thus came about a rapprochement between the English imperialists and the Indian bourgeoisie, which found its expression in the peaceful granting of formal independence by the British to a Congress-led India.[10]

Mel'man's thesis was generally supported by A. M. D'iakov, who denounced the British-Indian independence agreement as the result of collaboration between the imperialists and the Indian bourgeoisie. However, he suggested, a part of the bourgeoisie, chiefly those belonging to the ethnic minorities which were afraid of being swallowed up by the majority group, might join in the fight against the agreement.[11]

According to V. Balabushevich, the Indian bourgeoisie was trying to throw off the colonial yoke, but since at the same time it was attempting to serve its own interests by maintaining a colonial living standard for the

---

[8]   Zhukov, *K polozheniiu*, pp. 6-8.
[9]   Zhukov, *K polozheniiu*, p. 3.
[10] "Izuchenie Indii," *Vestnik Akademii Nauk SSSR*, (No. 8), 1947, p. 86. This article is a summary of the reports to the conference. The reports of Balabushevich, Mel'man, and D'iakov, the speakers most opposed to the Indian national bourgeoisie at the meeting, are given in full in Volume III of the *Uchennie zapiski* of the Pacific Institute. However, since this volume was not published until 1949, there is a possibility that the full reports may have been somewhat altered to bring them politically up to date.
[11] *Izuchenie Indii*, p. 88.

workers and preventing the rise of a powerful labor movement, not too much could be expected of it.[12]

We might wonder, in view of this unenthusiastic attitude expressed towards nationalist India, if there were any conditions under which a more friendly Soviet view towards India could develop. In his report to the conference, A. A. Guber suggested that there were, if the Indian nationalists followed the example of the Indonesians. Guber explained that whereas just after World War I the Indian National Congress had given inspiration to the Indonesian nationalists, after World War II Indonesia formed an example for India to follow. He emphasized that "although the attitude of the (Indian) bourgeoisie to the Indonesian independence struggle was a reserved one, it was the democratic masses of India which looked to the example of Indonesia, where it had proved possible to combine the struggle for national independence with a struggle for a radical social reform."[13]

Guber's remarks, which unfortunately we have only in their condensed version,[14] are interesting to us on three counts. In the first place, we see the Indonesian revolution again put forth as an exemplary type of national independence struggle. Secondly, we note that the reason given for the Indonesian Republic's superior nature was that the revolution was aimed not only at independence but a far-reaching social reform. The question naturally arises as to whether Guber considered, contrary to the normal pattern of Communist thought, that the bourgeoisie itself was leading a struggle for radical reform, or whether he felt that the far Left, rather than the bourgeois nationalists, had control of the revolution. Unfortunately, the summary of Guber's report which is available to us does not deal with this; but, as we shall see, Soviet comment came increasingly to assume that the latter was the case and eventually reached the surprising conclusion that Indonesia was a people's democracy. Guber's statement on the matter is of particular interest because it referred to an Indonesia still governed by Sutan Sjahrir, who, though the radical Left was well represented in his cabinet, was clearly not pro-Communist himself.

---

[12] *Izuchenie Indii*, pp. 88-89.

[13] *Izuchenie Indii*, p. 91.

[14] His discussion was omitted — understandably in view of what happened in 1948 — from the publication of the full reports two years later.

We might well inquire *as to* the nature of the "radical social reform" being pushed by *the* Indonesian Republic. If we do, we will be hard put to find any. Neither the Sjahrir nor the Sjarifuddin governments paid very much attention to internal reforms in this period, for the very good reason that they had their hands full with securing the Republic against the Dutch. No major land reform was carried out, large land-holdings being anyway almost wholly restricted to the princely territories of Djogjakarta and Surakarta. Foreign enterprises and land under lease to foreign-owned estates had been guaranteed by the Indonesian government under the Linggadjati Agreement, a concession supported by, among others, the Indonesian Communists. We must thus either assume that the Soviet political analysts were quite badly informed on the Indonesian domestic scene — which is by no means unlikely, to judge from the whole course of Soviet comment on Indonesia during this period — or look elsewhere for the real reason behind Soviet approval of the Republic.

There seem to be two obvious points at which the Indonesian situation differed from that of India. In the first place, the pro-Communist Left enjoyed what was apparently a much more favorable position in the Indonesian government than in the Indian. Secondly, Indonesia was engaged in a difficult and sometimes bloody struggle against its colonial master, whereas India had come to terms with Britain — a most suspicious act in Soviet eyes, and one which did not suit Russian interests at all. It is probably useless to ponder which of these two elements formed the basis of Soviet preference for the Indonesian over the Indian pattern; most likely both of them entered into it.

The conferences discussed above cannot be considered policymaking events, of course; but, inasmuch as Soviet political theory serves primarily to reflect and justify government policy, they seem symptomatic of the Soviet attitude towards the colonial question. The fact that they did not display the monolothic unity of argument so rigidly enforced in Stalinist Russia, and the fact that the differences in thought continued for some time are perhaps some indication that the Soviet policy-makers themselves did not know what line to take. Perhaps they found it unimportant, for the parts of Asia which this problem concerned were still a long way off in the Soviet view of things, and for a long time no decision was taken.

One of the few major points on which Soviet comment on Southeast Asia seemed *to be* agreed was its favorable view of Indonesia and Viet Nam. Sometimes Maoist China was added to the two republics as a major force in the Asian revolution; we learn that "only the growth of the national-liberation movement among the colonial peoples of Asia (especially in China, Indonesia, and the Indochinese peninsula) is a stumbling-block to the victory of the US monopolies in this continent."[15] In retaliation for Indonesia's opposition to American economic designs, the US was doing everything to destroy the Republic:

American government officials and diplomats are bending every effort to place the yoke of imperialist slavery once more on the Indonesian people and to assert themselves conclusively in this richest part of the globe. The Anglo-American reactionaries have sabotaged all the proposals of the Soviet representative and the representatives of other countries in the Security Council for a cessation of hostilities in Indonesia and for the granting to the Indonesian people of the right to arrange their own governmental existence as they see fit.[16]

In September 1947, with the establishment of the Cominform, the Soviet Union buried the last remnants of its wartime alliance. At the founding session of this body, it was stated that:

While the war was on, the Allied States in the war against Germany and Japan went together and comprised one camp. However, already during the war there were differences in the Allied camp as regards the definition of both war aims and the tasks of the post-war peace settlement...Two diametrically opposed political lines took shape: on the one side the policy of the USSR and the other democratic countries directed at undermining imperialism and consolidating democracy, and on the other side, the policy of the United States and Britain directed at strengthening imperialism and stifling democracy.

Under these circumstances it is necessary that the anti-imperialist, democratic camp should close its ranks, draw up an agreed program of actions and work out its own tactics against the main forces of the imperialist camp, against American imperialism and its British and

---

[15] B. M. *Shtein*, "*Poslevoennaia ekonomicheskaia ekspansiia SShA v Azii*," Vestnik Leningradskogo universiteta, (No. 10), *October 1947*, p. 64.

[16] "Razgrom Iaponskikh *imperialistov* i bor'ba za mir i bezopasnost' narodov na Vostoke," *Bol'shevik*, (No. 17), September 15, 1947, p. 6.

French alliance against the right-wing Socialists, primarily in Britain and France.

This imposes a special task on the Communist Parties. They must take into their hands the banner of defense of the national independence and sovereignty of their countries. If the Communist; Parties stick firmly to their positions, if they do not let themselves be intimidated and blackmailed, if they courageously safeguard democracy and the national sovereignty, liberty and independence of their countries, if in their struggle against attempts *to enslave their* countries economically and politically they will *be able to* take the lead of all the forces that are ready to fight for honour and national independence, no plan for the enslavement of the countries of Europe and Asia can be carried into effect.[17]

This "two camp doctrine" was propounded in greater detail by the Soviet spokesman, Andrei Zhdanov, who declared that:

This (anti-fascist) camp is based on the USSR and the new democracies. "It also includes countries that have broken with imperialism and have firmly set foot on the path of democratic development, such as Rumania, Hungary, and Finland. Indonesia and Viet Nam are associated with it; it has the sympathy of India, Egypt and Syria. The anti-imperialist camp is backed by the labour and democratic movement and by the fraternal Communist parties in all countries, by the fighters for national liberation in the colonies and dependencies, by all progressive and democratic forces in every country.[18]

The lack of importance ascribed to the Asian situation by Soviet thought at this time seems clearly evidenced in Zhdanov's speech, which, except for the above passage and a short paragraph observing the weakening hold of Western imperialism on Asia, ignored the colonial problem completely. His lengthy analysis of the two camp division does not supply us with any indication of a clear-cut Soviet attitude towards Asian nationalism. The special position of Indonesia and Viet Nam and the ignoring of China may

---

[17] "Declaration of the Conference of Representatives of the Communist Party of Yugoslavia, the Bulgarian Workers' Party (Communists), the Communist Party of Rumania, the Hungarian Communist Party, the Polish Workers' Party, the Communist Party of the Soviet Union (Bolsheviks), the Communist Party of France, the Communist Party of Czechoslovakia, and the Communist Party of Italy on the International Situation," *For a Lasting Peace, for a People's Democracy*, (No. 1), November 10, 1947, p. 1.

[18] A. Zhdanov, "The International Situation," *For a Lasting Peace, for a People's Democracy*, (No. 1), November 10, 1947, p. 2.

seem familiar to us, but Zhdanov's view of India, Egypt, and Syria appears much more sympathetic than that expressed by most Soviet analysts at that time. The most likely explanation for Zhdanov's mentioning of these three countries would seem to be that they were all engaged at the time in disputes of varying seriousness with Great Britain; that the statement had no real policy implication would seem indicated by the fact that Soviet journalistic comment on India did not shift towards a more favorable attitude. Zhdanov's speech, it would seem, gave an authoritative outline of the two camp doctrine only for Europe; and the formal adaptation of the concept to Asia was still to come.

With the adoption of the two camp doctrine, the moribund Varga theory was formally denounced[19] thus severing all ideological connections with the wartime alliance. Still, however, no hard and fast line for Asia was laid down. Then, in November, the Pacific Institute of the Academy of Sciences held a conference on the influence of the October Revolution on the countries of the East. As might be expected, most of the meeting's time was devoted to a portrayal of the Soviet Union as an inspiration and example for the Asian revolutions. Two reports, however, are worth observing in some detail.

An analysis of the Indonesian situation was presented by A. A. Guber, who apparently felt that he need have no hesitation in stating to which of the two camps the Republic belonged. "Today," he declared, "Indonesia belongs to the anti-imperialist front; the ideas of Lenin and Stalin have directed the Indonesian people in the struggle for independence and true democracy."[20] These are quite strong words, but, as we shall see, they were not atypical for the Soviet view of the Republic at this time.

Of considerable interest, too, is a report by G. V. Astaf'ev, who spoke on the Chinese concept of New Democracy. The political system of the new China, he explained, was original in that it consisted of a bloc of all democratic parties under the leadership of the Communist Party; and its economic system called for the existence of capitalist forms under socialist control, at least for the first period of revolutionary rule. Astaf'ev concluded that "the new democracy in China is a phenomenon

---

[19] The November 1947 issue of the *Kon'iunkturnii biulleten' mirovogo khoziaistva i mirovoi politiki* is devoted to this denunciation.

[20] "Velikaia oktiabr'skaia revoliutsiia i strani Vostoka," *Vestnik Akademii Nauk SSSR*, (No. 1), January 1948, p. 41.

of the universal development in the capitalist world of new, transitional systems, which, while retaining capitalist forms under public control, work towards the maturing of socialist elements with the goal of public ownership and collective forms of labor."[21]

Here is one of the first occasions in which the uniqueness and importance of the Chinese example was publicly observed in Soviet political analysis. It was important not only because it denoted a gradual appreciation of Chinese Communist power, but because it meant a break with the traditional view of the Communist role in the Asian revolution. As we have seen in Astaf'ev's analysis, the Soviet Union saw the key to Mao's New Democracy in the hegemony of the Communist Party over a broad united front which included various other anti-imperialist parties. Such an analysis combines a friendly attitude toward the national bourgeoisie — hitherto a characteristic of the united front from above — with the demand that the revolutionary movement be under the leadership of the Communists — a feature of the united front from below.[22] In effect, the new line was a declaration that the Communists themselves could lead a nationalist revolution based on a non-proletarian program of national independence, land reform, and economic modernization.

The further doctrinal differences between the Maoist and previous Soviet theories on the colonial question are too abstruse to tackle here, and one wonders whether or not they have any real significance. The major contribution of Maoism to Communist revolutionary thought is, it would seem, a matter of spirit more than of theory. We have observed the Soviet tendency to discount in actual practice the ability of Communists in colonial and semi-colonial regions to gain control of the nationalist movement and successfully lead the anti-imperialist revolution. Mao, however, had demonstrated that this was possible: relying on nationalism and the peasant's desire for land reform, he had seized the leadership of the Chinese revolution from a Kuomintang which could not answer the popular demand for equality, modernity, and swift, economic progress.

The realization that the Communists could in fact become the spokesmen for nationalism had, of course, a tremendous impact on the

---

[21] *Velikaia oktiabr'skaia revoliutsiia*, p. 41.

[22] Cf. Kautsky, *Moscow and the Communist Party of India, pp.* 17-24, for a further discussion of the difference between Chinese and Soviet Communism.

Soviet view of Asia and the role of the Communist parties in that area. It is this new self-confidence and assumption of the nationalist robe which, more than any other factor, has been the distinguishing mark of Asian Communism since the Chinese victory. It was, however, by no means a universal solution to the Communist tactical problem in underdeveloped areas. We have already remarked that the Soviet interpretation of the Maoist revolutionary strategy taught that the Communists should encourage nationalism and court the national bourgeoisie. On the other hand, however, it implied that the Communists must and could take control of the nationalist movement, either bringing the nationalist parties under their influence or destroying them. This program might be eminently successful in' countries where the ruling nationalist movement was weak and corrupt, as in China; but it presented a dilemma of no mean proportions in areas like India or Indonesia, where nationalist leadership was still strong and popular.

The Soviet interpretation of Maoism — which came to be known as the "national front" strategy — was not adopted by the USSR immediately upon its appreciation by some Russian political analysts; not until 1949 was the "Chinese way" officially declared the proper road for Asian Communism. Meanwhile, there remained two schools of thought. One, typified by China expert V. Maslennikov, pointed out the value of the Chinese example for the Asian revolution: "The peoples of Indonesia, Vietnam, Korea, who have not yet freed themselves from foreign dependence and the threat of colonial enslavement, who have not yet resolved the most important problems of the bourgeois-democratic revolution, are studying and putting into practice the magnificent experience of the construction in China of a new type of state."[23] Others, however, continued to look to the united front from below, with its rejection of the national bourgeoisie, for the proper Communist course in Asia. The two tendencies had one thing in common: both rejected collaboration with the leadership of non-Communist movements except on the basis of Communist domination. In practice, this meant that Communist tactics in the colonial countries began to turn sharply to the left, away from cooperation with the nationalist leaders.

---

[23] V. Maslennikov, "Bor'ba kitaiskogo naroda za natsional'nuiu nezavisimost' i svobodu," *Mirovoe khoziaistvo i mirovaia politika*, (No. 12), December 1947, p. 28.

The implications of the two camp doctrine for the Asian situation were first worked out authoritatively in an article by E. M. Zhukov which appeared in the party organ *Bol'shevik* in December, 1947. Zhukov showed himself to be an advocate of the Maoist line: he called for a broad front of revolutionary elements led by the Communist Party. Indonesia, he felt, was an excellent example of a state based on these tactics:

In a number of colonial and dependent countries a people's anti-imperialist front has been formed, consisting of a coalition of parties having the struggle for liberation as their platform, under the leading participation of the Communist Party (Indonesia, Viet Nam). The political program of such a coalition envisages complete independence from foreign imperialism and broad democratic reforms, laying the foundations for the economic and political independence of the country. Such a program must be aimed not only against imperialism, but also against its internal social backers — the landlords and that national bourgeoisie which is connected with foreign capital. It is well known that democratic forms have already been successfully put into practice in large areas of the liberated parts of China, in the unoccupied territory of the Indonesian Republic, and in the inner regions of the Republic of Viet Nam.[24]

Indonesia's progressive character and its similarity to Viet Nam are repeated frequently:

(The national liberation movement) encompassed Asia and Africa, and took especially sharp forms in such countries as China, Indonesia, Indochina... In Indonesia and Indochina there were born in the battle against imperialism new governmental forms — democratic republics. The Indonesian Republic *has* just the same progressive, democratic character (as Viet Nam(. It, too, was born in the fire of the struggle against Japanese imperialism. ...

In the same manner, the 90 million inhabitants of Indonesia and Viet Nam have refused to bow further to the system of colonial exploitation. They are courageously defending their right. ....[25]

Comrade Zhdanov remarked in his report that Indonesia and Viet Nam are associated with the anti-imperialist camp. ...The intervention

---

[24] E. Zhukov, "Obostrenie krizisa kolonial'noi sistemi," *Bol'shevik*, (No. 23), December 15, 1947, p. 57.

[25] Zhukov, *Obostrenie krizisa*, p. 52.

of the imperialists, pursuing colonial wars which have as their goal the destruction of the Indonesian Republic and Viet Nam, is an expression of the terror of the imperialists before the contagious strength of the examples of Indonesia and Viet Nam for other colonial peoples.[26]

Indonesia was thus placed firmly in the democratic camp. The picture painted here of an Indonesian revolution "under the leading participation of the Communist Party" is a strange one, but, as we have seen, it was a view voiced several times earlier on the Soviet side. This optimistic attitude towards the Republic reached its high point in an article in the foreign affairs journal *Voprosi ekonomiki* in the beginning of 1948. Here it was explained that "The broadness, strength, as well as the achievements of the national liberation struggle in each separate colonial country are determined by internal as well as external factors, to wit, the relationship of the moving forces of the national liberation movement to those which form the leadership of that movement at a given stage. The peoples of Indonesia and Viet Nam, entering into the advance guard of the liberation struggle of the colonial peoples, have formed people's democratic republics."[27]

The idea of Indonesia as a people's democracy is at first blush extraordinary; but it is in effect what Zhukov had implies in his analysis. The concept of people's democracy as it was developed to apply to the countries of East Europe called for the achievement of control over the bourgeois democratic revolution by Communist-led forces, so that the new state formed by the revolution would be not a bourgeois-democratic, capitalist one but a semi-socialist state which would develop under proletarian leadership towards socialism.

This term was later applied to post-revolutionary Communist China, creating some confusion, since the East European and Chinese situations differed considerably in some respects. At any rate, the application of the term to Indonesia would imply that the Indonesian revolution was considered to be proceeding under Communist hegemony; and it is made clear in the article under discussion that this is precisely what is intended:

The decisive role in this first stage has been played by a united national front on the broadest democratic basis, which was formed in the course

---

[26] Zhukov, *Obostrenie krizisa*, p. 57.

[26] V. Vasil'eva, "Bor'ba za demokraticheskoe razvitie Indonesiiskoi respubliki," *Voprosi ekonomiki*, (No. 1), 1948, p. 81.

of the struggle in Indonesia. All those parties and groups supporting the Republic have formed a coalition — the "National Concentration" — under the leadership of Sardjono, a prominent, active Communist, leader of the Communist Party.

The Indonesian united national front is not only a union of political parties and organizations, but is a very broad alliance of workers, millions of landless and land-poor peasants, the urban poor, craftsmen, and a part of the national bourgeoisie.[28]

We might well wonder, with an eye to what was to come in the near future, whether the Soviet Union rejected all compromise between the Indonesian people's democracy and the Dutch. This is not apparent, however, from Soviet comment at that time. The above-quoted article observed that the conclusion of the Linggadjati Agreement had been necessary in its time: "The signing of the Linggadjati Agreement between Holland and Indonesia in March 1947 established, though it by no means satisfied the Indonesians, a new order in Dutch-Indonesian relations. This agreement created an opportunity for the Republican government of Indonesia to engage to a considerable degree in the realization of practical plans of reconstruction." [29]Less sympathy was expressed for the Renville Agreement, which had just been negotiated with the aid of the UN Good Offices Committee; it was viewed as having been forced upon the reluctant Indonesians by United States pressure and the threat of renewed Dutch attack. This attitude was apparent in Soviet press comment during negotiation of the agreement, though it was nowhere declared flatly that the Indonesian government should not sign.

In large measure, the Indonesians shared the Soviet objections to the Renville Agreement; but, since the United States had indicated at the Renville discussions that it was likely to wash its hands of the Indonesian affair unless the Republic agreed to it, the Sjarifuddin government considered that the only choice was to sign. [30]In this it was supported only by the Left Wing: the major non-Communist parties, desiring stronger opposition to the Dutch and fearing growing Leftist strength and orientation towards Moscow, withdrew their support of the government and brought about Sjarifuddin's resignation (January 1948).

---

[27] Vasil'eva, *Bor'ba*, pp. 81-82.
[28] Vasil'eva, *Bor'ba*, p. 75.
[29] Kahin, *Nationalism and Revolution in Indonesia*,.p. 228.

Immediately on Sjarifuddin's loss of the premiership, President Sukarno appointed Vice President Mohammad Hatta to form a cabinet responsible to the President and not to Parliament, until some measure of political unity could be achieved. The new cabinet contained no representatives of the Sajap Kiri: what was more, a part of Sjarifuddin's own Socialist Party split off under the leadership of the right socialist Sutan Sjahrir, forming a new group (the Indonesian Socialist Party — PSI) which supported the Hatta government. Sjahrir's defection meant that the Sajap Kiri's parliamentary strength was severely cut and that it lost its former majority in the powerful Working Committee of Parliament. A revolution was thus achieved in the formal power relationships of the Indonesian parties; at one blow the Indonesian Left had lost its strength within the governmental structure, though outside the government its strength had been little affected.

If the USSR had considered Indonesia safely on the side of the Soviet camp — and Russian comment on the Republic had certainly given that impression — this sudden turn of events must have come as an unpleasant surprise. This was so at least for the author of the last-quoted article, who apparently learned the bad news just in time to attach the following paragraph to the account of Indonesian people's democracy:

The latest events taking place in Indonesia — the resignation of the Indonesian government and the formation of the rightist government under Mohammad Hatta, the majority of the members of which are of pro-American sympathy — bear witness to the direct intervention of Wall Street into the internal affairs of the Indonesian Republic. The Americans are attempting to unite reactionary groups from the Masjumi and National parties and are relying on them in their expansionist policy; but the mass of the people, the working class of Indonesia, is carrying on a struggle against the provocations of American imperialism. They are demanding the replacement of the pro-American government and the return of the government of the socialist Amir Sjarifuddin.[31]

---

[30]   Vasil'eva, Bor'ba, pp. 84-85.

CALCUTTA AND THE INTRANSIGENT LINE

In January 1948, a writer in the Soviet Communist journal *Party Life* gave assurance that "The Republican government and the democratic parties of Indonesia, including the Communist Party, do not cherish any illusions in regard to the mediating activities of the Commission of Three, and place their hopes instead on their people and the moral and political support of democratic forces the world over. ...In the face of the danger threatening the country from the side of the imperialists, the Communist Party of Indonesia, the people, and all the democratic forces of the country are exerting all their powers for the repulsion of the interveners and are honourably defending the freedom and independence of their republic."[1]

A few weeks later, just before the announcement of the formation of Hatta's cabinet, the TASS correspondent from Djakarta was to report that:

According to information from journalistic circles, the situation in Indonesia has become increasingly difficult as a result of the intervention of reactionary US circles. They point out that the fall of the Sjarifuddin government took place under the direct influence of Wall Street.

Through their representative in the Three Power Commission, the Americans are trying to bring together reactionary groups from both the Masjumi and Nationalist parties in order to create in them a base from which to introduce the expansionist policy of Wall Street into Indonesia. They draw attention to the fact that the American representative in the Three Power Commission has recently been holding lengthy discussions with Masjumi leaders, in particular with Sukiman, and also with leaders of

---

[1] I. Plishevskii, "Kommunisticheskaia partii Indonezii boretsia za svobodu i nezavisimost' svoei strani," *Partiinaia zhizn'*,No. 1, January 1948. The article was presumably written sometime in January, since it refers to events taking place in the beginning of that month.

the Nationalist Party whose pro-American attitudes are well-known. The Americans are trying to remove from political activity the left socialists, Communists, and members of other democratic organization.[2]

The Americans succeeded in their "plot," apparently, for on February 2 *Pravda* found itself forced to announce the creation of a cabinet composed of pro-American elements, formed under the influence of the Three Power Commission, which was personally directed by Graham, the American member of the committee." On February 6, the paper declared that "the situation in Indonesia has become strained since the American imperialists succeeded in removing the government of Amir Sjarifuddin and creating a cabinet of extreme rightist pro-American elements," and it spoke of mass demonstrations in the Republic demanding Sjarifuddin's return.

Sjarifuddin did not regain his post, however; and both the Soviet Union and the Indonesian Communists found themselves faced with the problem of reviewing their attitude towards the Indonesian government. Heretofore support of the Indonesian government, defense of the Republic, the struggle against the imperialist camp, and the drive for Communist hegemony in Indonesia could be seen as one, for they were not patently incompatible aims. Now, however, that unity had broken down, and the Communists had to develop a system of priorities for its various components. The struggle against the "imperialist camp" — the Western bloc — was of course the prime concern for the Soviet Union. Since the USSR was gaining considerable propaganda benefits from its support of the Republic in the UN, it faced the problem of whether it should continue to support the Indonesian government even at the expense of sacrificing Indonesian Communist hopes for power. If the Communists were to oppose the regime, on the other hand, how far should their criticism of the government go: should it be a loyal opposition or should it take a more drastic form?

These were fundamental questions of policy and, even though Indonesia was not a problem of major importance to the Soviet Union, they were not likely to be solved in a day, the more so since it was not at all clear for some time after Hatta had come to office that his government was anything more than a temporary makeshift which would remain

---

[2] *Pravda*, January 30, 1948.

in power only until some sort of agreement had been reached among the contending major parties. Nonetheless, there has been considerable speculation that the Indonesian Communist uprising of September 1948 had been ordered by the Soviet Union within a few weeks after the formation of the Hatta government, when the USSR was supposed to have commanded the various Southeast Asian Communist, risings which were to take place that year. The central argument of this theory focuses about a Communist-sponsored Southeast Asian youth conference held in Calcutta in February; here, it is claimed, "orders from Moscow" were passed to the Southeast Asian Communists dictating the rebellions in Indonesia, Malaya, and Burma and the increased unrest in the Philippines and Viet Nam which occurred later in 1948. The writer is not adept enough at distinguishing fact from fancy to attempt a discussion of the secret liaisons of international Communism in this paper; but since the theory concerning the Calcutta conference had received considerable acceptance, it might be well to devote some space to that meeting and its possible significance for the Indonesian question.

The major contacts between the Indonesian Left and international Communist-oriented organizations were through the World Federation of Trade Unions, to which the Indonesian labor federation SOBSI had belonged since the spring of 1947, and the World Federation of Democratic Youth (WFDY), to which the general Indonesian youth organization, the BKPRI, was affiliated.[3] In February 1947, four WFDY representatives arrived in India; they were to travel through various Southeast Asian countries to survey the colonial situation there and make contacts with youth organizations in the area.[4] The commission was able to take

---

[3] The first congress of the WFDY, held in London in November, 1945, was attended by nine Indonesian students who had been in the Netherlands throughout the war; they included Maruto Darusman and Suripno, who not long after rose to important posts in the Indonesian Communist Party. Suripno was made a member of the WFDY Council at that time. Indonesian representatives also attended the founding congress of the International Union of Students, held in Prague in 1946. It should be noted, however, that neither these organizations nor the WFTU were frankly Communist at their inception, though pro-Communist elements quickly gained control of them. Most of the non-Communist members dropped out during 1946 and 1947; and after the Czech coup in February 1948 there was practically no non-Communist European membership. Since the leadership of the WFDY, IUS, and WFTU passed into Communist hands quite soon after their establishment, the views of these organizations in the period we are dealing with expressed quite consistently the international Communist line.

[4] According to the WFDY, the commission was supposed to set off in November 1946 but was delayed by the outbreak of hostilities in Viet Nam and the refusal of the French authorities to grant permission to enter Indochina. The delegation finally consisted of four representatives, Olga

advantage of the Indian-sponsored Inter-Asian Relations Conference in New Delhi to make contact with Southeast Asian representatives to that meeting. In April, the WFDY group held a meeting with some of the younger delegates to the conference; it was attended by eight Indonesian representatives, including Suripno and Maruto Darusman.[5] It was decided at this discussion that a full-scale Asian youth conference should be held in the near future.[6] The Indonesians, under Suripno's leadership, volunteered to play host to the projected meeting, and the conference was duly scheduled to be held in Indonesia some time in November.[7]

At the Delhi meeting, the Indonesians extended an invitation to the WFDY commission to visit their country, which it did in May.[8] The delegation was treated impressively by both government and general populace, the Indonesians being eager for any chance to gain sympathy for their cause. The WFDY representatives met with Sukarno, Hatta, Sjarifuddin, Wikana, and a number of other political and labor leaders.[9] Their enthusiasm was apparently aroused, for the report they made to the June 1947 meeting of the WFDY executive in Moscow stated that "freedom and democratic rights have been brought by the young Republic,"[10] and that progressive youth was playing a major role in Indonesia's affairs. "We saw their enthusiasm and that of the whole nation, when we accompanied the President of the Republic on one of his journeys to the West of the country," the delegation declared.[11]

Following the Delhi meeting, the WFDY and IUS sent a joint invitation to all youth and student organizations in the Far East to attend

---

Chechetkina, a Soviet journalist who has specialized in Southeast Asia, Jean Lautissier, a WFDY leader who later played a key role in the Calcutta Conference, Rajko Tomovic from Yugoslavia, and M. O. Oleson from Denmark. (*Report of the WFDY Commission to South East Asia*, WFDY, mimeographed, n.d. (1948(, p. 1).

[5]   WFDY *Information Service*, May 15, 1947, p. 2.

[6]   According to the WFDY, the conference was proposed by the Burmese representatives (*Report of the WFDY Commission*, p. 1), though this does not, of course, preclude the possibility that the WFDY delegation had had this in mind itself or encouraged the Burmese in their proposal.

[7]   WFDY *Information Service*, May 15, 1947, p. 2; July 1, 1947, p. 4.

[8]   Cf. Charles Wolf, *The Indonesian Story*, (New York, 1948), pp. 85-86; Suripno, "Indonesian Students and International World," *Merdeka*, New Delhi, (No. 26), February 21, 1948, p. 9;and the *Report of the WFDY Commission*. The Danish delegate, *M..O.* Oleson, did not accompany the rest of the WFDY group to Indonesia.

[9]   *Report of the WFDY Commission*, p. 2.

[10]   *Report of the WFDY Commission*, p. 12.

[11]   *Report of the WFDY Commission*, p. 13.

the Asian youth conference.[12] At the June executive meeting it was, however, decided to limit the scope of the conference to Southeast Asia. We shall not go into the further details of the conference's preparations, save to note that the Indonesians, having made plans to hold the meeting in the Javanese city of Madiun, found themselves disappointed when, in an executive meeting held after its World Youth Festival in July 1947, the WFDY decided that the Dutch attack on the Republic, which had taken place several weeks previously, made the situation too uncertain to hold a conference there. It was therefore decided to hold the meeting in Calcutta and, finally, to postpone it until the middle of February, 1948.[13]

It thus came about that the Southeast Asia Youth Conference was the first international Communist-oriented public meeting at which the Southeast Asian countries were represented after the promulgation of the two camp doctrine, From the published reports of the conference, it is clear that a very strong emphasis was placed on the two camp concept. It should not, however, be assumed that this meeting was necessarily the first time the Southeast

Asian Communists were made aware of the new line; the Indian party, for example, had already adopted it in a meeting of its central committee held in December 1947.[14]

Whether or not the conference's analysis was something new for the Southeast Asian Communists, it is of considerable interest to us here as an example of the developing international Communist attitude towards nationalism and colonialism:

The end of the Second World War saw the biggest revolutionary upsurge in the countries of South East Asia, symbolized in the setting up of the Republics of Viet Nam and Indonesia. In other countries like India, Pakistan, Burma, and Ceylon, the imperialists, unable to crush the postwar revolutionary upsurge changed their tactics and with the help of right wing leadership announced concessions, which was nothing more than a sharing of power with local reaction and compromising leadership. In those countries, the Government, dominated by the right wing and acting as the trustees of the vested interests, are calling upon the people to concentrate on reconstructing the country, and in the name of reconstruction are

---

[12] *Jeunesse du monde*, (WFDY), (No. 6), 1947, p. 23.
[13] Cf. WFDY Information Service, October 1, 1947, p. 6.
[14] Cf. Kautsky, *Moscow and the Indian Communist Party*, pp. 82-89.

busy in giving all help to vested interests and suppressing the democratic struggle of the people for better living and for land.[15]

"Neither reforms nor so-called reconstruction within the framework of colonial exploitation" would be enough it was asserted; what was necessary was the "total defeat of imperialism and its allies."[16]

From these excerpts we can draw several important conclusions. First of all, it is apparent that the Communists had by now decided that the "neutralist" countries of Asia were to be placed in the imperialist camp, and it was therefore the duty of the Southeast Asian parties to oppose them and their attempts at internal reform. Secondly, it is clear that the Indonesian Republic was not considered to be in this neutralist category. Quite the contrary; it was declared that "the peoples of South East Asia desire their total independence; …the Vietnamese and Indonesian Republics are living examples before their eyes."[17] The secret of Indonesian and Vietnamese success seemed in total, armed opposition to the imperialists: "In Indonesia and in Viet Nam the highest form of armed struggle has been attained. The people of these countries have known the meaning of foreign domination and, having once tasted independence, cannot tolerate a new enslavement. Partisan warfare has been organized and is everywhere in progress."[18]

This emphasis on armed action had been growing in Communist accounts of the colonial situation since the promulgation of the two camp doctrine; we see it, for instance, in a previously cited article of January, 1948, praising the Sjarifuddin regime.

Fully characteristic for Indonesia is that situation about which comrade Zhdanov spoke in his report when he emphasized that the peoples of the colonies do not wish to live as they did before, that the ruling classes of the metropolis can no longer run the colonies as they did before, and

[15] *Hands Off South East Asia.* Conference of the Youth and Students of South East Asia-Fighting for Freedom and Independence, Calcutta, February 19-28, 1948. Special bulletin of the Colonial Bureau of the I. U. S., (No. 1), Praha, April 1948, p. 29.

[16] "Quittez l'Asie' Lachez prise," *La Jeunesse Combat le Colonialisme*, (Colonial Bureau of the WFDY), (No. 1), 1948, p. 5. A WFDY report on the conference.

[17] Jean Lautissier, Arrachons a griffe etrangere!" *Jeunesse du Monde*, (No. 8), 1948, p. 12. This is a report by the chief WFDY delegate to the conference. Cf. also Lautissier, "A la vielle de Conference d'Asie du Sud-Est," *Jeunesse du Monde*, (No. 7), July 1948, p. 8.

[18] "Rapport principal concernant la situation de la jeunesse en Asie du Sud-Est et son combat qu'il mene contre l'imperialisme, pour la liberte, l'independance, la paix, contre le danger d'une troisieme guerre mondiale," *La Jeunesse Combat le Colonialisme*, (No. 1, 1948), p. 11. The main report to the conference, presented by the Vietnamese delegation.

that the attempts of the imperialists to suppress the national liberation movement by military might is meeting up with a steadily growing armed resistance by the colonial peoples, giving rise to protracted colonial wars. Such a war is indeed taking place right now in Indonesia.[19]

If this praise of armed revolution is to be interpreted as a Soviet hint to the Southeast Asian Communists-which may be stretching the point a bit far, just as American praise of the recent Hungarian revolt did not necessarily indicate US encouragement of the rebellion-it would naturally have serious implications for Communist parties in colonial countries like Malaya, or in countries whose governments were living on friendly terms with the Western powers, such as India, Burma, and the Philippines. It cannot be applied directly to the Communist rebellion that took place later in Indonesia, however, for, as we have seen, the Republic was specifically declared at this time to be on the side of the angels.

We cannot give any certain answer as to why the Calcutta meeting did not place Indonesia in the same category as India, Burma, and the Philippines, since an unfavorable attitude would seem indicated by the gloomy Soviet comments on the Hatta government. It may be that the leaders of the conference, none of whom were major Communist figures, were still following the line of several weeks before, when the Hatta cabinet was still unformed. It may also have been caused by a Soviet decision to play down its disapproval of the new cabinet in view of its propaganda investment in Indonesia in the United Nations. Indeed, the Indonesian question was even then being debated in that august platform for political harangues, Gromyko roundly condemning the Committee of Good Offices report to the Security Council on the Renville Agreement and defending the Republic at inordinate length against what he considered to be the machinations of the Western imperialists.

That a conscious effort was made to de-emphasize Russian differences with the Indonesian government would seem indicated by the fact that, after its first flurry of indignation at the establishment of the Hatta government, the unfavorable Soviet comment ceased. The last critical remarks in *Pravda* were made on February 29, when the paper noted that "as a result of lengthy secret pourparlers with bourgeois nationalists in Indonesia, Graham was able to name a new cabinet, into which entered

---

[19] Plishevskii, *Kommunisticheskaia partiia Indonezii*, p. 65.

ministers of pro-American sympathy." After that, directly unfavorable comment on the Republican government was laid aside until August, 1948; in the interim, both the Soviet and Dutch Communist press devoted their coverage of Indonesia to praise of the Republic in its struggle against the Dutch. The Indonesian government itself was carefully ignored: attention was instead devoted to the Republic as a symbol of the anti-colonial struggle. In this manner the Soviet Union managed to support the Republic in the name of anti-colonialism without explicitly supporting the Republic's non-leftist government.

This division was clearly an artificial one, a makeshift that was likely to prove unstable, particularly in view of the increasingly strict interpretation of the two camp doctrine voiced by the Soviet Union. That dogma's rejection of all compromise with imperialism had an immediate effect on the Communist view of the Republic's negotiations with the Dutch. The main resolution of the Calcutta Conference declared that "Thanks to the American-dominated 'Good Offices Commission' of the United Nations, the Dutch have succeeded in imposing an agreement on Indonesia which ensures the continuation of the Netherlands colonial regime over the people of Indonesia, and at the same time, opens the door to American penetration."[20] The Indonesian delegates to the meeting announced their opposition to the agreement and their desire to continue combat against the Dutch,[21] at which sentiments the conference expressed its satisfaction: "The prestige of Indonesia, won through two and a half years of heroic struggle against the Dutch went up, when the Indonesian delegate in unequivocal terms declared that Indonesian youth will continue the fight for final independence despite the truce, signed between the Indonesian and Dutch Governments, under pressure of the Three Powers Commission, dominated by American imperialism."[22]

Whether or not the Calcutta Conference served any important function in passing along Soviet directives to the Southeast Asian Communist parties, it would seem fairly safe to consider the views propounded in its resolutions as expressive of the international Communist attitude towards the Southeast Asian situation; if we accept this, we come to the conclusion that what was being advocated by the USSR was not direct opposition to

---

[20] *Hands Off South East Asia*, p. 32.

[21] Lautissier, *Arrachons a griffe etrangere!*, p. 12.

[22] *Hands Off South East Asia*, p. 4.

the Republic and its government as such but a sterner attitude towards negotiations with the Dutch. Some evidence for this would seem to be provided by the subsequent absence of Soviet criticism of the Hatta government and by the fact that shortly after the Calcutta meeting the Sajap Kiri, re-organizing itself into the People's Democratic Front (FDR), denounced both the Linggadjati and Renville agreements, for which it had previously been the principal Indonesian advocate.[23]

While this emphasis on a more militant stand against the Netherlands may not have been directly aimed at destroying relations between the Indonesian government and the Left, it did have this effect in the long run. Nearly any responsible Indonesian government, realizing the precarious international position of the Republic, would find itself forced to deal with the Dutch and to recognize the need for concessions, even as Sjarifuddin and Sjahrir had previously. With the country splitting more and more decidedly into pro-Soviet and non-Soviet blocs, such a government might very well view with alarm the expansion of an aggressive Left Wing whose very entrance into the government might tip the scale of US opinion against the Republic and thus lose Indonesia its vitally needed American sympathy in the UN. The pro-Communist Left, for its part, found itself forced by the two camp doctrine and the deepening cold war to insist with increasing emphasis on the necessity for the Republic's alignment with the Soviet bloc and on the government's firm resistance to the Western imperialists. When the Hatta government refused this and showed no desire to allow any increase in the Left's voice in the government, the Indonesian Communist Party (PKI) had to reconsider: should the fiction of a Republic engaged in an uncompromising fight against Western domination be preserved, or should it be acknowledged that the Indonesian government was no more satisfactory to the Communists than was the Indian? The decision was a long time in coming, and it was so bound up with the course of

---

[23] While one is naturally inclined to consider the reversal of the Leftist line to be a reflection of the new Communist attitude towards compromise with the Dutch, it should in fairness be noted that, since the concessions were generally unpopular, there was a natural tendency for the parties out of power to oppose them. Thus, while the Sjarifuddin government had been defeated ostensibly because it concluded the Renville Agreement, the opposition parties, on coming into power, realized the Republic had no alternative and supported the pact, while the Sajap Kiri(FDR took the more popular but irresponsible position of opposing it. The interpretation of the FDR's change in attitude as being a reflection of the international Communist line should therefore be accepted with certain reservation.

events within the country that it is impossible to say where the domestic power struggle ended and the international one began. In increasing measure, however, the conflicts within the Republic were determined by the deepening of the cold war, and compromises became less and less possible as the country divided into two alien camps. In the end, the conflict which was so disadvantageous to both sides was brought about; and to this extent perhaps the cold war and the two camp doctrine can be considered to be responsible for the September rebellion.

THE SURIPNO AFFAIR

During the spring of 1948 the two factions into which Indonesian political forces had divided made strenuous efforts to arrive at some sort of compromise, for they were well aware of the danger of not presenting a united front to the Dutch. By May there were signs that an agreement might indeed be achieved: it was announced that the government would be re-organized on the basis of a broad National Program that had been accepted by all parties. Hatta would remain premier, but the Left would enter the cabinet; Alimin announced that the Communists would take part in the government. On May 26, however, the Soviet Union made an announcement that buried for good all hope of an effective compromise.

As we have previously noted, Soviet public comment on the Indonesian situation had carefully avoided any criticism of the Republic after the end of February. True, there was some mention of American intrigues with "reactionary circles" in Indonesian politics, but these were not specifically identified with the Hatta regime. The only sign of any change in the Soviet point of view was Indonesia's absence, from February on, from the front ranks of the national liberation movement in Russian and Cominform comment. Vietnam, and, increasingly, China were cited as the pattern for the Asian revolution, while the Republic faded into the background.

The Soviet Union, however, had apparently not taken the Left's reversal in Indonesian politics as lightly as its public attitude would suggest: for on May 26 it suddenly announced that an agreement had been initialled between the Soviet Union and the Republic's representative in Prague for an exchange of consuls between the USSR and Indonesia.[1] The first

---

[1] Cf. *Pravda*, May 26, 1948; *De Waarheid*, May 26, 1948; *Lukisan Revolusi*, p. 326. Some other sources, such as the *Christian Science Monitor*, July 23, 1948; S. P. Derita, *Lima Minggu sebelum Madiun Affair* (Medan, n.d.), p. 8; and Virginia Thompson and Richard Adloff, *The Left Wing in*

reaction on the part of the Indonesian government was surprise; the next was shock, as the implications of the announcement for the Republic's domestic and international position became clear. The story of how the agreement came to be made is still very much a mystery; but from the reports which have been pieced together, the following-perhaps inaccurate-account emerges.

Suripno, who initialled the agreement on behalf of the Republic, was a member of the PKI Central Committee; he had left Indonesia for Prague in the summer of 1947 to attend a WFDY congress.[2] With the authorization of Foreign Minister Hadji Agus Salim, he remained in that city as Indonesian envoy to East Europe and set up a Republican information office there.[3] In November he approached M. A. Silin, the Soviet ambassador to Czechoslovakia, in an effort to secure Soviet recognition of Indonesia; he also brought up the matter with representatives of the governments of the people's democracies.[4] The response of the Soviet representative was encouraging, and Suripno requested authorization from the Republic to conclude an agreement with the Soviet Union. On December 25, Sukarno granted him authorization to come to an agreement with the Soviet government for the establishment of consular relations.[5]

By January 13, Suripno had received the Republic's instructions , and he immediately opened negotiations with Silin[6] Agreement was

---

Southeast Asia (New York, 1950), give the date as May 27; this very likely refers to the date the announcement became known in the Republic.

[2]   Statement by Hadji Agus Salim, Radio Jogja broadcasting in Indonesian, May 27, 1948; Netherlands radio (Hilversum), broadcasting in Dutch to Indonesia, May 27, 1948.

[3]   Statement by Hadji Agus Salim (Radio Netherlands, Hilversum, broadcasting in Dutch to Indonesia, May 27, 1948). In this statement, the Foreign Minister emphasized that he had not authorized Suripno at that time to conclude any agreements on behalf of the Republic.

[4]   Mirajadi, "Tiga Tahun Provokasi Madiun," Bintang Merah (VII, 12(13), August(September, 1951, p.49. This is the PKI version. According to Kahin, Nationalism and Revolution, p. 268, Suripno told him that he had approached the Soviet ambassador in January 1948, It would seem likely, however, in view of the apparent fact that Suripno requested and received authorization from the Indonesian government in December 1947 to conclude consular exchange agreements, that he had had some contact with the USSR concerning the matter prior to this.

[5]   Pravda, June 8, 1948; De Waarheid, May 20, 1948; Christian Science Monitor, July 23, 1948. The Indonesian delegation to the discussions then taking place between the Dutch and Indonesians at Kaliurang announced that Suripno had been given a general mandate in December 1947 to establish consular relations with Central and East European countries in connection with the threat of resumed Dutch military operations against the Republic (Radio Jogja, English language broadcast, May 29, 1948).

[6]   Statement to the press by Suripno (Radio Jogja, August 13, 1948).

reached quickly, and in the same month a pact for the exchange of consular representatives was initialled by the two negotiators. Suripno then asked the Republic for further instructions. At that time, however, the Sjarifuddin government was in the midst of the Renville discussions, and it was felt by the Indonesians that an agreement with the Soviet Union at that point would have an unfortunate effect on the negotiations, especially as regards the American attitude towards them. The pact was thus shelved; and the succeeding Hatta government refused to bring the matter back to life. The Soviet government finally decided to take things into its own hands, however, and on May 22 it informed Suripno that it had ratified the consular agreement.[7]

According to a statement made by Suripno on returning to Indonesia, he had opened negotiations directly on receipt of the Republic's mandate, but "owing to unforeseen circumstances" the agreement could not be signed until May 22 (Radio Jogja, August 13, 1948).

We do not know what the motives of the Soviet government were in so suddenly bringing to a head the consular issue, though several reasonable explanations are available. It may perhaps have been that Russia, having observed the fall of the Sjarifuddin government and the subsequent unfavorable political development of the Republic, may have felt a need for closer contact with the Indonesian situation. Consular representation in the Republic would serve to keep the Soviet Union better informed of developments in Indonesia, and a closer guidance of Communist activities there would be possible. In addition, Soviet relations with the Republic might serve as a counterweight to that country's dependence on American good will and would strengthen the Soviet Union's claim to

---

[7]   Kahin, *Nationalism and Revolution*, p. 268; citing an interview with Suripno. The official Soviet version is given in the announcement of the agreement:
"Some time ago the special representative of the Government of the Indonesian Republic, Minister Plenipotentiary Suripno, addressed himself in the name of the Government of the Indonesian Republic to the Soviet Government through the Embassy of the USSR in Prague with a proposal for the establishment of relations between the Soviet Union and the Indonesian Republic
"As a result of discussions taking place in Prague between the two Governments, an agreement was concluded for the establishment of consular relations and an exchange of consuls between the Soviet Union and the Indonesian Republic.
"The agreement that had been reached was ratified by an exchange of letters between USSR Ambassador to Prague M. A. Silin and Envoy Extraordinary and Minister Plenipotentiary of the Indonesian Republic Dr. Suripno.
"The exchange of letters took place on May 22 on the premises of the Soviet Embassy in Prague." (*Pravda*, May 26, 1948.)

be the true defender of the Indonesian cause. It is also possible that the Soviet Union, which by now had lost all tolerance of Asian neutralism, had decided that it was high time to call a showdown with the Republic and demand that the Indonesians declare themselves as allies or enemies of the Russian camp.

Whatever the Soviet motives may have been, the USSR's announcement placed the Hatta government in a most embarrassing position, as the Russians must have known it would. Officially, the Indonesian government was committed to an independent foreign policy and had declared it would welcome diplomatic relations with all nations. Refusal to accept the agreement would further alienate the Left and could be used by it to persuade the people that the Hatta government was, after all, a puppet of the United States. On the other hand, the government realized that the Republic was to a great extent dependent on American good will, which it feared would be transferred to the Dutch if the US considered the Indonesians were in danger of becoming too friendly to Communism. The Dutch, for their part, found the situation an ideal barrel over which to place the Republic, and they loudly proclaimed that the Renville Agreement — which they interpreted to forbid an extension of Indonesian foreign relations — had been violated and that the Republic had now given proof of its Communist leanings.

We shall not describe the Indonesian attempts to deal with the situation beyond remarking that, after a confusing round of denials and explanations, the government called Suripno home from Prague on the grounds that it desired a further explanation of the agreement. Until then, the question of relations with the Soviet Union was to be shelved. It was quite obvious, however, that the government, in spite of its brave declarations on the independence of its foreign policy, was somewhat less than enthusiastic about concluding an agreement with the Russians. Hatta, indeed, went so far as to state publicly that any agreement Suripno had made would not be submitted to Parliament if it involved an extension of Indonesia's foreign relations.[8] In this the government was supported by the Masjumi and Nationalist parties, while the FDR, having at first hailed the agreement as a political triumph for the Republic, bitterly condemned Hatta's stand.

---

[8]   *Christian Science Monitor*, July 23, 1948; Radio Jogja, English-language broadcast, June 1, 1948.

From this point on, the problem created by the polarization of Indonesian political life began to assume a hopeless aspect. Attempts were still made at achieving a compromise; but it was increasingly evident that they were mere gestures, made to absolve one faction or the other from the guilt of sabotaging the revolution. In all too short a time it became apparent that, unless a solution were somehow achieved, relations between the government and opposition would break down completely.

Curiously enough, the Soviet Union did not react to its rejection by the Republic by roundly condemning the Indonesian government, though, since the Russians had given considerable publicity to the conclusion of the consular agreement, the situation must have been somewhat embarrassing for them. Publicly, at least, the Russians excused the Republic on the grounds that it had been forced to abandon an agreement it actually wanted, as a result of Dutch and American pressure:

These are the facts. They clearly point out who is trying to hinder the establishment of friendly relations between the USSR and the Indonesian Republic. Completely clear, too, are the motives lying at the root of the base behavior of the representatives of the USA and Holland in Indonesia. They are prepared to allow only those foreign relations to the Indonesian Republic which they would keep under their control.[9]

This tolerant attitude is all the more striking in view of the fact that Communist dogma had by this time lost all sympathy for Asian neutralism and had at times identified it bluntly with black reaction. In the Cominform journal of the time one could read of "the reactionary governments of Spain, Greece, Portugal, Argentina, India, and other."[10]

While no certain statement can be made as to the reason for this forbearance, it may perhaps be seen as some evidence for the argument that the Soviet Union intended the consular agreement less as a showdown with the Indonesian government than as an attempt to gain some sort of outpost in the Republic.[11] There were, of course, the considerable

---

[9]   *Pravda*, June 8, 1948.

[10] Guiseppe di Vittoria, "WFTU — Results EC Meeting," *For a Lasting Peace, for a People's Democracy*, No. 11 (14), June 1, 1948, p. 5.

[11] Further evidence for this thesis may possibly be found in the fact that Suripno, on his return to Indonesia, declared that the agreement did not imply *de jure* recognition of the Republic by the Soviet Union. The question of whether the consular agreement would represent such recognition had been a source of concern to the Republican government, since a refusal of recognition, while

benefits gained by Soviet propaganda from the United Nations situation as another factor militating against a Soviet quarrel with the Republic. And it may be that Russia considered something might still be salvaged for the Communist cause in Indonesia; though by now it should have been disillusioned as to the government's willingness to allow any considerable growth in Soviet influence. At any rate, both Soviet and Dutch Communist press comment returned after the Suripno affair to the same line of comment they had carried before it; and for another two months no clouds appeared to trouble the bright blue sky of Soviet admiration for Indonesia.

While all this was going on, however, developments were taking place in the ideological field which were to have an important effect on the Soviet view of Indonesian nationalism.

In China, as 1948 wore on, the Communist forces scored increasingly important victories over the tottering Nationalist regime. Given the standstill to which Communism was brought in Europe in that year, we would expect that the Soviet Union would have devoted particular attention to the rising red star in the East. There was, indeed, increasing publicity given to the Chinese Communist victories, and sometimes speeches by Chinese Communist leaders were reported at length in the Cominform and Soviet press; but on the whole it appears that the Soviet Union was extraordinarily cautious in accepting the implications of the Chinese revolution.

It has been claimed by some — most notably by Mr. Khrushchev in his denunciation of Stalin at the twentieth CPSU congress — that a factor behind the USSR's hesitancy regarding the Chinese Communists was that, in Stalin's eyes, Mao's independence from Soviet tutelage represented a threat to Russian pre-eminence in the Communist world. Whether this was the case or not, the USSR's attitude in 1948 towards

---

it would have been necessary if the promise not to expand Indonesian foreign relations were to be kept, would have been extremely unpopular. A consular exchange without recognition could possibly take place within the limits of the Dutch interpretation of the Renville Agreement, though it would not have as much value as far as propaganda towards the Indonesian people was concerned. This might thus indicate that the Soviet Union was more interested in actually obtaining a consular arrangement than in propaganda. If the exchange were accepted, Suripno declared, other East European countries would propose consular exchanges. The agreement, he said, represented a first step towards achieving trade and economic relations with the Soviet bloc, with *de jure* recognition as the eventual goal. (Suripno, in a press interview, as reported in Merdeka, August 14, 1948, p. 1).

movements independent of the Soviet orbit — Communist or otherwise — was unfavorable indeed. We have seen how the two camp doctrine was interpreted more and more stringently, until there was no room left for a nation to be "democratic" and still independent of the Soviet camp. Then, in June 1948, the USSR's position as autarch of the Communist world was struck a blow which brought the Cominform to declare itself even more strongly against that force which impelled most strongly towards independence:

The Resolution of the Information Bureau of the Communist Parties declares that the roots of the mistakes made by the leaders of the Communist Party of Yugoslavia must be sought in the undoubted fact that nationalist elements... dominate in the leadership, and that the leadership of the Yugoslav Party, having broken with the international traditions of the Communist Party of Yugoslavia, has taken the path of nationalism.[12]

Tito's break with the Cominform came as a deep shock to the Soviet Union: it had not been thought possible that even so popular a leader as he would be able to defy the Russian will successfully.

The Soviet reaction was immediate and hysterical in its suppression of independent elements in other East European Communist parties. Some, like Poland's Gomulka, were lucky enough to be imprisoned; others, like Hungary's Rajk, were not permitted to live to benefit from a future change in the party line.

It was not only in East Europe, however, that the purge of Titoist elements was carried on; nationalism everywhere, whether within or without the Communist movement, was declared anathema:

Nationalism as the ideology of the bourgeoisie is the enemy of Marxism. They (The Titoists) must realize that Marxism-Leninism cannot reconcile itself with nationalism, or with any nationalist deviation in the Communist Parties; that it must destroy nationalism in whatever form it arises for the sake of the interests of the working people, for the sake of the freedom and friendship of the peoples, for the sake of the victorious building of socialism.[13]

---

[12] Vasile Luca, "Petty-bourgeois Nationalist Outlook of Yugoslav Communist Party Leadership," *For a Lasting peace*, No. 15 (18), August 1, 1948, p. 3.

[13] *Pravda*, September 8, 1948; quoted in *For a Lasting Peace*, September 15, p. 2. Cf. also *For a Lasting Peace*, September 15,1948, p. 3; December 1, 1948, p. 1; December 15, 1948, p. 2.

The Communist parties must be internationalist; as leaders in the proletarian struggle they cannot compromise with nationalism, for "the class content alike of opportunism and nationalism, is one or another form of agreement or rapprochement with the bourgeoisie."[14] And the key to true internationalism is allegiance to the Soviet Union:

The Bolshevik Party has always considered that the interests of building socialism in the Soviet Union completely merge with the interests of the revolutionary movement in all countries. ...

Bourgeois nationalism is manifested in the strivings to weaken the bonds of friendship with the Soviet Union: it reflects the influence of foreign imperialist reaction and the class enemy inside the country. The attitude toward the Soviet Union is now the test of the devotion to the cause of proletarian internationalism, of willingness to put the Lenin-Stalin doctrine on the national question into practice for this doctrine is an integral part of the general question of socialist revolution.[15]

This argument, *frank to the point of* brutality, brought the *two camp doctrine to the extreme towards* which it had been pro*gressing during the year of its* existence. It was not the *socialist nature of a country's economy nor* its refusal of alliance with *the West that mattered: the sole* criterion was subservience *to the Soviet Union*. As *can* readily be imagined, such an interpretation applied to Indonesia would make support of the Republic by the Communists impossible *except at terms* that would mean civil war.

The condemnation of nationalism brought with it the necessity of evaluating anew the relationship of the Communist movement to the class struggle in the colonial countries. Only a year or *two before, we will remember, the* bourgeois nationalists had been viewed as allies of the Communists in the struggle for national liberation in colonial areas. As we have seen, however, Communist sympathy for the nationalist bourgeoisie had died since that time in those countries where the

---

[14] Boleslav Beirut, "*For Complete Elimination of Right and Nationalist Deviation,*" For a Lasting *Peace,* No. 18 (21), September 15,1948, p. 3.

[15] "Struggle against Bourgeois Nationalism — Most Important Task of Communist and Workers' Parties," For a Lasting Peace, No. 23 (26), December 1, 1948, p. 1. Another version of the same theme: "In view of the growing polarisation of forces on a world scale between the imperialist and anti-imperialist camp, now more than ever before, the attitude toward the USSR becomes the touchstone of genuine internationalism, of loyalty to the cause of socialism, and, at the same time, the firm and sole bulwark of our independence and sovereignty." (Boleslaw Beirut, For Complete Elimination of Right and Nationalist Deviation, p. 3).

nationalist governments had come to a peaceful agreement with the colonial powers. Indonesia remained the only Asian country where the Communists had continued to support a bourgeois nationalism that was not under their control. That support was already badly strained, however; and the declaration against nationalism in the summer of 1948 forced the PKI to break with the nationalist cause entirely or somehow reconcile it to the new Soviet dictum.

There were two possible approaches on the basis of the demand for loyalty to the USSR to the problem presented by bourgeois nationalism. The first possibility was a return to the strict class approach of the classical left strategy, with its complete rejection of the nationalist bourgeoisie. This interpretation would seem supported by the emphasis placed in Soviet and Cominform writing of the period on the necessity of combining the proletarian struggle with the fight for national liberation: "Just like the exponents of the 'third force', Tito's petty-bourgeois, nationalist group confuses — in a bourgeois sense — the interests of the working class and the working peasantry with the interests of the nation; it ignores the existence of antagonistic classes and the sharpening of the class struggle in Yugoslavia and thus denies the danger of the rebirth of capitalism in the country."[16]

This *view* was *expressed with* particular frequency in comments on the Indian *situation, the* Soviet Union having come to take an especially *sour view of that* country's nationalist movement: "The Indian masses *are now convinced* on the basis of their experience that the bourgeoisie *does not desire* and is not capable of achieving in a consistently democratic manner the complete independence of the country, the elimination of all vestiges of the feudalism which is shackling its development, and the solution of the national (minorities) problem." [17]

The second possibility was that propounded by Mao Tse-tung, who was urging at that time a united front composed of "workers, peasants, artisans, professional people, intelligentsia, the liberal bourgeoisie and a part of the gentry who have split off from the landlord class. This we call the 'broad mass of the people."[18]Far from being repudiated,

[16] Luca, *Petty-Bourgeois* Nationalist *Outlook*, p. 3.
[17] A. M. D'iakov, *Natsional'nii vopros i angliiskii imperializm v Indii* (n.p., 1948), p. 34.
[18] Mao Tse-tung, "Agrarian Policy of the Communist Party of China,"address to cadres of the Shansi-Suiuan Liberated Area, *For a Lasting Peace*, No. 13 (16), July 1, 1948, p. 6.

the national bourgeoisie was courted; the Communists emphasized the "importance of extending both public and private economy in the liberated territories, and urged the public sector to give more help to the private enterprises."[19]

There was, however, one condition which the national bourgeoisie must meet to be considered part of the democratic movement — it must accept the leadership of the Communist Party. This would mean a struggle against bourgeois democratic groups which refused Communist leadership and an insistence that the nationalist bourgeoisie resign from control of the national revolution. The bourgeoisie, with the whole of the liberation movement, must "lean to one side," in Maoist parlance: it must declare its allegiance to the Soviet camp.

No attempt was made to resolve the important doctrinal difference between the interpretations offered for the Indian and Chinese situation;[20] but as far as Indonesia's immediate future was concerned, it made little difference. Both the Maoist and the orthodox leftist views demanded Communist leadership of the revolution; both rejected cooperation with non-Communist movements on a basis of equality. Either interpretation, injected into the Indonesian situation in the summer of 1948, was bound to have explosive consequences.

There was another sense in which the reaction to Tito was to have an important effect on the political situation in the Republic. Following Tito's desertion, the Soviet Union, apparently fearing the infectious influence of nationalism, laid heavy stress on the demand that the Communist Party dominate any mass movement in which it might participate. Such a requirement would be bound to have

---

[19] "Progress of Industry and Trading in Liberated Territories in North China," *For a Lasting Peace*, No. 17 (20), September 1,1948, p. 2.

[20] On the contrary; Cominform and Soviet pronouncements in reaction to Tito and in support of the East European collectivization drive at times took what might seem to be an anti-Maoist line:
Concerning the leading role of the working class, the leaders of the Yugoslav Communist Party, by affirming that the peasantry is the "most stable foundation of the Yugoslav state" are departing from the Marxist-Leninist path and are taking the path of a populist, kulak party. Lenin taught that the proletariat is the "only class in contemporary society which is revolutionary to the end... must be the leader in the struggle of the entire people for a thorough democratic transformation, in the struggle of all working people and the exploited against the oppressors and exploiters. ("Resolution of the Information Bureau Concerning the Situation in the Communist Party of Yugoslavia," *For a Lasting Peace*, No. 13 (18), July 1, 1948, p. 1).
Tito, of course, relied on the peasantry much less than did Mao.

important consequences for the Indonesian leftist coalition, where the Communists shared control with elements that could not be relied on to follow the Soviet line. Consider the Cominform's criticism of the Yugoslav People's Front; it might well have been applied to the FDR by some irate proletarian puritan:

The Information Bureau considers that the leadership of the Communist Party of Yugoslavia is revising the Marxist-Leninist teachings about the Party. According to the theory of Marxism-Leninism, the Party is the main, guiding and leading force in the country, which has its own, specific programme, and does not dissolve itself among the non-Party masses. The Party is the highest form of organization and the most important weapon of the working class.

In Yugoslavia, however, the People's Front, and not the Communist Party, is considered to be the main leading force in the country. The Yugoslav leaders belittle the role of the Communist Party and actually dissolve the Party in the non-party People's Front, which is composed of the most varied class elements (workers, peasants engaged in individual farming, kulaks, traders, small manufacturers, bourgeois intelligentsia, etc) as well as mixed political groups which include certain bourgeois parties. The Yugoslav leaders stubbornly refuse to recognize the falseness of their tenet that the Communist Party of Yugoslavia allegedly cannot and should not have its own specific programme and that it should be satisfied with the programme of the People's Front.

The fact that in Yugoslavia it is only the People's Front which figures in the political arena, while the Party and its organizations does not appear openly before the people in its own name, not only belittles the role of the Party in the political life of the country, but also undermines the Party as an independent political force, which has the task of winning the growing confidence of the people and of influencing ever broader masses of the working people by open political activity and open propaganda of its views and programme.[21]

It is interesting to note that this viewpoint, while it had no other relation to Maoism, had the effect of bringing the Soviet line closer to

---

[21] "Resolution of the Information Bureau Concerning the Situation in the Communist Party of Yugoslavia," *For a Lasting Peace*, No. 13 (18), July 1, 1948, p. 1. Cf. also "The Communist Parties — the Vanguard Detachment of the Working People," For a Lasting Peace, No. 11 (14), June 1, 1948, p. 1.

the Chinese on an important principle: the necessity of Communist hegemony over the mass movement.

With these developments in mind, we shall turn to Indonesia in August 1948 and the return of one of its prodigal sons.

REVISION AND REBELLION

On August 11, Suripno finally arrived back in the Republic. No doubt the Indonesian government had awaited his arrival with some misgivings, but they certainly did not bargain for what they got. With Suripno, disguised as his secretary, came an Indonesian Communist leader who had been living in the Soviet Union since his flight from the Indies nearly twenty-five years before. His name was Musso; he had been one of the early leaders in the revolutionary movement, and as such had considerable prestige among the Indonesians. In addition, he claimed to have returned to Indonesia in 1935 for a year in order to establish an underground Communist Party; if his claims to this and to the illegal organization's membership are true, he was already the acknowledged leader of a number of the more prominent figures in the FDR.

Musso immediately took command of the PKI and announced a major revision of its composition and policy, a change which was carried out with far-reaching effects on the Indonesian political situation. We have generally avoided a discussion of internal Indonesian developments so far, but since Musso had undoubtedly returned to the Republic at Russia's behest and with a program outlined in Moscow, a general discussion of his reform should be of no little interest to us here.[1] It should be kept in

---

[1] Since documents dating from this period of Indonesian history are few and far from reliable, it might be well to note briefly here the sources used in reconstructing Musso's program. The major statement embodying the Communist leader's ideas is *Djalan Baru untuk Republik Indonesia* (The New Road for the Indonesian Republic), a resolution passed by the PKI Politburo in August 1948 in response to Musso's criticisms of the Party, It was first printed in the September 1948 issue of *Bintang Merah*, the Communist Party journal. Unfortunately, the writer has been unable to obtain a copy of this issue and has had to rely on later reprints of the speech issued by the Indonesian Communist Party. It is possible, of course, that these have been subjected to some revision from the original, though so far I have found no evidence of this.

The second principal source for Musso's program is Lima *Minggu sebelum Madiun Affair*, a collection of speeches and press interviews, almost all by Musso, as reported in Republican newspapers of the period. It was published in Medan in 1949 by an Indonesian calling himself

mind by the reader, however, that we cannot be sure Musso did not add to or alter his Soviet instructions after arriving in Indonesia; and therefore we cannot consider the policies instituted by him as an absolutely reliable indication of the Soviet program for the Republic.

Musso's arrival in Indonesia was greeted with mixed feelings on the part of the non-Communists, if we may judge from reports of the period. On the one hand there was, of course, a feeling that his coming meant trouble. On the other side, a hopeful segment of opinion expressed the thought that he might be a *deus ex machina* who would somehow resolve the alarming domestic conflict. And at first it did appear as if Musso had this in mind: one of his first actions was to criticize the FDR-sponsored strike wave, which had just led to a serious clash between government and pro-Communist forces: "At a time like this, when reaction is gathering its forces to attack our Republic, it must be considered that from the point of view of unity such actions must be prohibited, in a way which will remove the factors dissatisfying the workers. And this problem must be settled in a peaceful manner, for the enemy can make use of every absence of peace in the country."[2] On being asked by President Sukarno to lend his support to the Republic and its revolution, he is said to have replied, "Indeed, that is my task. I have come back to set things straight."[3]

It was very soon apparent, however, that Musso's ideas on how to set things straight differed considerably from those of the Indonesian government. He came forth with a program which he quite frankly labelled

S. P. Derita. Where it has been possible to check the articles reprinted in Derita's booklet with those from newspapers of the time there has been no sign of any alteration in content. On the whole, both *Djalan Baru* and the reports in *Lima Minggu sebelum Madiun Affair* do not seem to deviate from available accounts of PKI policy published at the time of Musso's activity in the Republic; however, the writer has tried to give references, when relying on these or other later sources, to newspaper accounts contemporary to Musso's reform. Unfortunately, this has not been possible in the case of some of the more theoretical points-understandably, since the Indonesian newspapers were chiefly interested in Musso's views on foreign policy and the inter-party struggle. For the theoretical issues, and unfortunately these are among the most important for this paper, the reader will have to let his own judgment be his guide.

[2]   "Robah kabinet sekarang djadi kabinet Front Nasional," *Suara Ibu Kota*, August 14, 1948; in Derita, *Lima Minggu sebelum Madiun Affair* (Medan, 1949), p. 28. Cf. also Musso's interview with the newspaper *Buruh*,as reported in *Merdeka* (the chief nationalist newspaper of the time), August 16, 1948, p. 2; "Communist and Socialist Parties Merge," *Merdeka* (No. 42,September 5, 1948; this journal *Merdeka* was a publication of the Indonesian Republic information office in New Delhi), p. 8; "Communist Rising in Indonesia," *Merdeka* (New Delhi, No. 44),September 25, 1948, p. 5.

[3]   *Aidit Accuses Madiun Affair* (Djakarta, 1955), p. 26. According to another PKI source, Musso made his reply in good colonial Dutch: "Ik kom hier om orde te scheppen." (*Buku Putih tentang Peristiwa Madiun* (n.p., 1954), p. 7.) Cf. also *Merdeka*,August 16, 1948, p.2.

his "Gottwald Plan,"[4] aimed at a peaceful assumption of power by the
Communists in the manner of the Czech coup. His first action was to re-
organize the PKI along lines which, as we shall see, were in conformity with
the Cominform criticism inspired by the Titoist revolt. The Communist
Party, he maintained, should be the leading force in the national revolution;
but the PKI had allowed itself to drift with the nationalist tide and as a result
had lost control of the revolution. This was the same mistake that the West
European Communists had made after World War II; like them, the PKI
had submitted to bourgeois domination and had not asserted itself as the
leader of the proletarian movement. The PKI's Politburo, outlining Musso's
program towards the end of August, declared:

In the field of foreign policy, the Politburo meeting is of the opinion
that the great mistakes made by the Indonesian Communists during
these three years have not been accidental but have had their roots in the
events following the outbreak of World War II and the occupation of our
homeland by Japan; later they were influenced by the mistaken policy
of our brother parties, namely the West European Communist parties
(France, England, and the Netherlands). ...After World War II had
ended with the defeat of the three fascist countries, there was no longer
any reason for the Communist Parties in the capitalist and imperialist
countries and for the revolutionary forces in the colonial lands to continue
to cooperate with their governments. This was even more true after it had
become clear that the bourgeoisie had begun to take steps to suppress the
liberation movement in the colonial countries.

The mistake of the French and English Communist Parties, and
also of the Netherlands Communist Party, which was influenced by the
Communist Party of France, arose from a failure to understand the great
transformation which had taken place in international politics since the
world war, especially as regards the liberation struggle of the peoples of
the colonial countries...

Because of its failure to understand this change in the political situation,
the CPN (the Dutch Communist Party) held the view that the struggle of
the Indonesian people could not go beyond the limits of dominion status;
and because of this they claimed the slogan best suited for Indonesia was

---

[4]   Kahin, *Nationalism and Revolution*, p. 275. Suripno also used the Czech example in referring to the
PKI's new course (speech to the BKPRI, August 14; as reported in *Merdeka*, August 17, 1948, p. 2).

"Union ties," or, in other words, that Indonesia remain within the Dutch "Commonwealth" sphere. There Indonesian people were thus to continue to "cooperate" with Dutch imperialism. This was the same stand-point taken by the French Communist Party toward the Vietnamese liberation struggle.

This reformist policy was put into practice by comrades, former members of the CPN who came to Indonesia; they did this automatically and without careful consideration, and, moreover, without adapting it to the objective situation (the independence proclamation of August 17, 1945), with results that have endangered the success of our National Revolution.

It must be stated that this imported reformist policy gave a clear opportunity for the spread of the reformist wing, which took over the foreign policy of the Republic under the leadership of the right socialists (Sutan Sjahrir).[5]

Instead of forming a single working-class party after World War II, the Indonesian Communists had allowed the leadership of the Left to be spread over a number of loosely united groups, which weakened the party's position and confused the people. All this must now be remedied by a major organizational reform:

In connection with the mistakes in the principle of its organization mentioned above, and taking good notice of the lesson provided by events in Yugoslavia, the meeting of the PKI Politburo has decided *to institute a radical change* which has as its aim:

1. the return of the PKI to its position of leader of the working class as soon as possible.
2. the swiftest possible return of the good PKI tradition of the period before and during World War II.
3. the achievement by the PKI of HEGEMONY...in the leadership of the National Revolution.[6]

---

[5] Djalan Baru untuk Republik Indonesia (Djakarta, 1953), pp. 15-19. Cf. also "Kongres Koreksi Serikat Buruh Gula," Solo, September 8, 1948; in Derita, *Lima Minggu*, p. 37; also reported in Merdeka, September 13, 1948, p. 1. Statement of the central executive of SOBSI, Buruh, September 3, 1948; quoted in Kahin, Nationalism and Revolution, pp. 279-280. Buruh, September 14, 1948, p. 1. Declaration of the Socialist Party on joining the PKI, as reported in Merdeka, September 1, 1948, p. 1.

[6] *Djalan Baru*, p. 11. Cf. also *Merdeka*, September 1, 1948, p. 1; Buruh, September 14, 1948, p.1.

The proposed organizational revision took the form of a proposal to merge the components of the FDR-the Socialist Party, Labor Party, Socialist Youth (Pesindo), and the trade union federation SOBSI-into an enlarged Communist Party. Sjarifuddin, Setiadjit, Wikana, Abdulmadjid, and Tan Ling Djie, the key leaders of the non-Communist FDR groups, now announced they had been secret members of the PKI all along;[7] luckily, we shall not have to enter here into a discussion of the various theories as to whether or not they really had been. The various FDR components began to hold meetings and rallies to ratify their entrance into the Communist Party and to gain support for their action. It was clear that, once the reorganization had been completed, the Communist Party would emerge as an immensely powerful force and, as far as the government was concerned, a threat of no mean proportions.

What was even more menacing, however, was the revolutionary program which Musso proclaimed for the Republic. The Communist Party, he declared, must hold the leadership of the national revolution. It had been a grievous mistake for Amir Sjarifuddin to have so peacefully laid down the reins of government:

A very important error was the fact that the Amir Sjarifuddin cabinet resigned voluntarily, without offering any resistance whatsoever. The Communists at this time did not remember the admonition of Lenin: "The primary question in any revolution is the question of state power." With the fall of the Amir Sjarifuddin cabinet the way was opened for elements of the compradore bourgeoisie to seize control of governmental leadership and thus of the leadership of our National Revolution, while the Communists isolated themselves in the opposition. It may be said that from that movement on our National Revolution has been in great danger, a danger that has grown with the passing of time. Since that moment our National Revolution has been more and more clearly sinking into the pit of capitulation to Dutch and other imperialisms, a result of the very reactionary policy of compromise followed by the Indonesian bourgeois elements which took over governmental leadership.[8]

The Communists must regain control of the government and the revolution; and as a vehicle for this, the PKI proposed the establishment

---

[7] Cf. Kahin, *Nationalism and Revolution*, pp. 272-275.

[8] *Djalan Baru*, pp. 19-20. Cf. also *Merdeka*, September 13, 1948,p. 1 (report of a speech by Amir Sjarifuddin to the congress of the Sugar Workers' Union, Solo, September 7).

of a National Front, a broad coalition to be headed by the Communist Party:

The PKI is *convinced* that at this moment the Party of the working class cannot alone accomplish the bourgeois democratic revolution, and for this reason the PKI must work together with other parties. The Communists have, of course, taken action to achieve unity with the members of other parties and organizations. The sole (acceptable) form of this sort of union is the NATIONAL FRONT. The PKI must take the initiative in forming it, and the PKI must also play the leading role in it. This in no way means that the Communists will force other parties or individuals to follow them, but, on the contrary, the PKI must patiently convince all honest people that the only road to security is the formation of a National Front which is supported by all progressive and anti-imperialist people. *Every Communist must be truly convinced that without a National Front victory cannot be achieved. ...*

A genuine National Front must be formed from below; all members of parties which have agreed to the National Front must enter it individually. In addition, an opportunity is given to the thousands of progressive people who are without party affiliation to participate in the National Front. The committees of the National Front, both locally and at the center, must be elected from below in a democratic manner. In this way the National Front, once it is founded, will not easily fail, since it will no longer be overly dependent on the desires of the party leaders. In this way, the National Front will also make possible a lessening of political differences and will reduce opposition to a minimum.

At the same time, the PKI must do its best to see that the present government is replaced as quickly as possible with a responsible NATIONAL FRONT government which is based on the national program.[9]

The structure of the National Front was familiar enough to those who knew something of the Communist-led "coalitions" which existed in East

[9]   *Djalan Baru*, pp. 31-33. Cf. also "Usul Kompromi Mesti Ditolak," *Suara Ibu Kota*, August 14, 1948; in Derita, *Lima Minggu*, p. 25; "Saja Datang, Saja Lihat, dan...?" *Madjallah Merdeka* (I, 35), September 11, 1948, p. 6; and Musso, interview with the newspaper *Revolusioner*, reported in *Merdeka*, August 16, 1948, p. 2. For a more detailed outline of the structure of the National Front organization, cf. "Usul2 tentang Front Nasional," *Buruh*, August 16, 1948; in Derita, *Lima Minggu*, pp. 25-27; and Musso, interview with *Revolusioner*, August 14, as reported in *Merdeka*, August 18, 1948, p. 2.

Europe and China at the time; needless to say, the leadership of the major non-Communist parties in the Republic showed no enthusiasm for it.

The PKI laid down a number of demands on the government in behalf of its new mass movement, the most important of which, from the point of view of the non-Communists, was the desire that the government be purged of all elements that were not "truly anti-colonial."[10] Most interesting for our study, however, is the attitude towards the different economic classes expressed in the new doctrine; for in this we can perhaps see whether Musso's program tended towards the orthodox leftist line or the Maoist analysis.

The Communists declared that the Indonesian revolution was a "NATIONAL REVOLUTION or BOURGEOIS DEMOCRATIC REVOLUTION OF A NEW TYPE, a preparatory step to a higher form of revolution, the Socialist or Proletarian Revolution."[11] The phraseology sounds Maoist, for the idea that a Communist-led national revolt constituted a new type of bourgeois-democratic revolution was first put forth by the Chinese leader. But let us continue before drawing any conclusions as to Musso's orientation.

Although the revolution is a bourgeois democratic one, Musso considered, the bourgeoisie cannot lead it because of its tendency to defect to the imperialist camp: "The leadership of this revolution, although (The revolt) is still bourgeois in nature, cannot rightly be in the hands of bourgeois elements, but must be controlled by the workers. ... The existence of the countries of the new democracy in East Europe and the rise of the national revolution all over Asia points out clearly that the national bourgeoisie is no longer capable of leading a consistent anti-imperialist liberation movement."[12] However, this does not mean that the bourgeoisie should be eliminated:

Our revolution is at the present time of a NATIONAL type. It is truly a bourgeois democratic revolution. It still contains bourgeois elements.

---

[10] For a listing of the various PKI National Front demands, cf. *Djalan Baru*, pp. 26-30; *Merdeka*, August 18, 1948, p. 2; a resolution adopted by the SOBSI, in *Buruh*, August 23, 1948, quoted in Kahin, Nationalism and Revolution, pp. 277-278.

[11] Djalan Baru, p. 31.

[12] Musso, "Sifat Revolusi Kita," Revolusioner, September 5, 1948;in Derita, Lima Minggu, p. 21. Cf. also "Pemerintah Repoeblik moengkinkah didjatoehkan oleh golongan Kommunis?" Santapan Rakjat (I, 100), September 4, 1948, p. 1, citing *Keng Po* of August 23, 1948; statement by the SOBSI executive, *Buruh*, September 3, 1948, quoted in Kahin, *Nationalism and* Revolution, p. 279; Buruh, September 14, 1948, p. 1.

In certain cases, moreover, it may find itself forced to encourage the growth of these elements in order that with their help it may further the development of the country's economy. This does not mean, however, that capitalism should be allowed to progress to the extent that it can go over to the formation of cartels or trusts, so that in the end it will be able to control the economic and political life of the country. Capitalism can exist, *and moreover in the beginning must exist*, but only under State control and with its development checked so that it cannot return the country to a capitalist state. It is quite essential to allow the development of such a controlled capitalism. This is required because an agrarian land like Indonesia, which at the beginning of the revolution does not yet have sufficient means of production to stand alone, cannot, without the aid of such controlled private capital, improve the economy of the country so as to establish the basis for the higher revolution, the *proletarian or* socialist revolution.[13]

This would seem a distinctly Maoist interpretation, an impression which is further strengthened by Musso's analysis of the role of the various economic classes in the national revolution. He seemed to have doubts, however, about the present revolutionary value of the national bourgeoisie:

Other groups (besides the proletariat) which are democratic in nature are the peasants, especially the poor peasants and small peasants. The middle peasants must also be considered to be of a democratic nature. Among the rich peasants there were also some who at the beginning of the revolution held anti-imperialist sentiments. Among the national bourgeois elements, too, there were those who at the beginning of the revolution were of anti-imperialist feeling.[14]

As regards the peasant question, Musso took a clearly Maoist line in urging that the poor peasant be given land, that the middle peasant's rights be defended, and that the land of the rich peasants be confiscated completely if they have opposed the revolution and in part if they have supported it. Such a system of reform had been carried out, he asserted, in China and Czechoslovakia.[15]

---

[13]   Musso, *Sifat Revolusi,* p. 19.

[14]   Musso, *Sifat Revolusi,* p. 21.

[15]   Musso, Sifat Revolusi, pp. 19-20. Cf. also the SOBSI resolution of August 22, *Buruh,* August 23, 1948; quoted in Kahin, *Nationalism and Revolution,* p. 278; and *Merdeka,* August 24,1948, p. 1. The PKI resolution, *Djalan Baru,* however, expressed a viewpoint that can only be explained as an addition by the Indonesian Communists to the imported theory: The PKI policy for the peasants

It would seem, then, that Musso's program, if it was not consciously Maoist in its inspiration, was at least sufficiently similar to the Chinese line to ensure a general conformation on important theoretical points. We may speculate as to whether Musso's advocacy of a rather Maoist program indicates that the Russians, sending him back to Indonesia, had sufficient interest in the non-quite-accepted line to charge him with implementing it in Indonesia; it must remain, however, only a speculation.

As was to be expected in the light of Soviet policy in the summer of 1948, Musso's arrival brought no more pliable attitude on the part of the Left as regards negotiations with the Dutch. The Communists' prior support of the agreements was labelled the product of a mistaken continuance of the wartime policy of cooperation with the West, and it was emphasized that even under the most favorable circumstances the PKI would refuse to adopt a conciliatory attitude:

The Communists repudiate the Linggadjati and Renville agreements, not because Holland has proved unfaithful to them and has trampled these agreements to the ground. No! By no means! The Communists repudiate the Linggadjati and Renville agreements *on principle*, because these agreements, if put into practice, would create a state which in reality would be under foreign domination, which would differ from India, Burma, the Philippines and other foreign-dominated lands only in its name. Because of this the PKI firmly puts forth as its slogan: "Complete independence."[16]

---

in all Indonesia is: "Land for the peasantry." Thus every peasant must be given land, so that he can really feel to have gained by the revolution. However, the Communists must understand that at present and for some years to come it will not be possible to carry out this slogan because of the shortage of land on Java and Madura, and the excessively large number of peasants. Therefore, for the time being, the peasantry will be better helped by not dividing among them the lands which accrue to them as a result of the abolition of feudal forms in the agrarian sector. Rather, this land will be handed over to the village, and it will be the village which will regulate the allocation of this land and decide on the requests of the peasants (for the use of the land) in a manner which will bene fit them. (Djalan Baru, p. 29).

This would seem to be a response by the Indonesian Communists to the traditional Javanese communal control of land, which appeared so much closer to the Communist goal than did the prescribed slogan of land to the individual peasant. No doubt the PKI did feel somewhat at a loss in adapting international Communist ideas on the peasant question, since there was little large landownership in Indonesia, nor was there a significant class of rich peasants. At any rate, the Indonesian Communists, while they have admitted the prime importance of the peasantry to the national revolution, have down to the present time tended rather to slide over the agrarian problem when it came down to practice.

It might also be noted that the FDR(PKI was quite explicit in denying accusations that it desired the nationalization or socialization of the peasants' rice-lands (Cf. Buruh, September 14, 1948).

16 *Djalan Baru*, p. 23. Cf. also the SOBSI resolution of August 22,in *Buruh*, August 23, 1948, and quoted in Kahin, Nationalism and Revolution, p. 278, and Merdeka, August 24, 1948, p. 1

"We must now struggle like the Greek Communists, like the Chinese Communists, and that is in a consistently anti-imperialist manner. We do not want an independence like that of Nehru's country," Setiadjit declared.[17] Such resolutions could only mean an all-out military struggle with the Dutch, and the Communists made it clear that they fully recognized this implication:

The weakness of our revolution has been in general that it has been of a defensive nature from the very beginning. According to FRIEDRICH ENGELS, a very great revolutionary strategist, a defensive revolution has no possible hope of success.

In the long run, therefore, a revolution must be of an offensive nature; though it is true that a defensive revolution can achieve successes on a small scale.

People MUST NOT continually complain, "We have no weapons." There are weapons enough in the hands of the Dutch. Because of this we will, I hope, act according to the admonition of DANTON: "Courage, courage, and yet more courage."[18]

It would probably not be unreasonable to attribute at least part of the inspiration for the program of all-out offense to Soviet encouragement, since the USSR had already made it clear that its admiration for the Republic lay in the fact that it was fighting the Dutch. Both from the point of view of military harrassment of the West and of general propaganda value, the Soviet Union stood to gain by a break-down of the Indonesian-Dutch truce; while, to judge from the Russian estimate of neutralism at that time, the USSR would have preferred to see a vanquished but restive Indonesia to a Republic on the lines of Nehru's India. Nonetheless, it would be stretching things a bit too far to maintain that the whole idea of an offensive against the Dutch was a result of "orders from Moscow." There was a not inconsiderable body of public opinion in the Republic itself which, weary of unsuccessful negotiations and the chaos caused by war conditions and the Dutch blockade, was desperate enough to desire a showdown. It was this group to which the

[17] "Nasionalisir zonder Kompensasi," Jogja, September 11, 1948; in Derita, Lima Minggu, p. 42.

[18] Musso, "Untuk zelfkritik dalam Revolusi Nasional," Buruh, August 16, 1948; in Derita, Lima Minggu, p. 25. Cf. also Saja Datang, Saja Lihat, dan...?, p. 6; speech by Musso before the Jogja association of university students, as reported by the Antara (Indonesian nationalist)) news service, September 6, 1948; interview between Musso and the newspaper Revolusioner, as reported in Merdeka, August 16, 1948, p. 2.

opposition in the Republic had generally appealed and to which the Left itself had turned since its fall from office. The government, however, felt it had something more to fear from the Dutch than fear itself; and it could only have been deeply alarmed at Musso's insistence on an immediate all-out offensive.

There remained the very important question of the Republic's foreign policy under the two camp doctrine; and the PKI lost no time in stating its position. Alliance with the Soviet bloc was essential:

The Communists who allowed the growth and domination of this reactionary (neutralist) policy, both following it and giving it support, have made two mistakes:

a. They have forgotten the teachings of our revolutionary theory, to the effect that the anti-imperialist National Revolution has in the present day become a part of the world Proletarian Revolution. …The USSR, as the largest and strongest anti-imperialist force, must be looked on as a base, as a mighty fortress, or as a leader and vanguard in the anti-imperialist struggle all over the world. For there are only two camps in the world, which are opposed to each other, the imperialist and the anti-imperialist camps. For the Indonesian National Revolution *there is no other place than the anti-imperialist camp*!

b. The second mistake is that they have not understood well enough the relationship of power between the Soviet Union and Anglo-American imperialism in the time since the Soviet Union's swift success in occupying all Manchuria. It was already clear then that the position of the Soviet Union as the strongest force on the Asian continent, with a greater military power than US, English, and Australian imperialism, presented a good opportunity for the Indonesian people to begin its revolution. At this time the Indonesian Communists exaggerated the strength of Dutch and other imperialisms and underestimated the strength of the Indonesian Revolution as well as that of the other anti-imperialist forces.[19]

---

[19] *Djalan Baru*, pp. 15-19. Cf. also the statement of the SOBSI executive, *Buruh*, September 3, 1948; quoted in Kahin, *Nationalism and Revolution*, pp. 279-280; "Rusia Tidak Mengakui Kedaulatan Belanda," Suara Ibu Kota, August 14, 1948, in Derita, *Lima Minggu*, pp. 32-33; Musso's reply to

The Republic should not be so fearful of America, the Communists declared; the US was a paper dragon, and both the PKI and Indonesia as a whole had been fooled by American propaganda into making unnecessary concessions.[20] If, however, the Republic allied with the Soviet Union, it would find a support the imperial powers would not dare defy:

In its policy towards the Soviet Union, the PKI most strongly urges the establishment of direct relations between the Indonesian Republic and the Soviet Union in all areas. The Soviet Union is an indispensable ally for the Indonesian people against imperialism, for the Soviet Union is the vanguard of the struggle against the imperialist bloc, which is led by the United States. It is clear enough that the United States is helping and making use of the Netherlands to smash our democratic Republic. The PKI must explain to the masses that Soviet recognition is an unmixed blessing, for the Soviet Union as a workers' state cannot have other than an *anti-imperialist* standpoint. The Soviet Union therefore has no interests as regards Indonesia other than helping it in its anti-imperialist struggle.[21]

Considerable emphasis was placed on the benefits of Soviet friendship by the Indonesian Left in the National Front campaign. The USSR itself reportedly contributed to the pressure for the establishment of connections between Indonesia and Russia by approaching Indonesian representatives in Bangkok through its legation there with suggestions for trade between the two countries.[22] Whether this is true or not, the idea that the USSR would send ships through the Dutch blockade and thus relieve the Republic's desperate economic situation was certainly not discouraged by the Indonesian Communists: "As for Holland, a country as small as that will not dare to stop Russian ships; and America, too, will have respect for the Republic if it knows that behind the Republic

---

Hatta's speech before Parliament of September 2, as reported by Merdeka, September 6, 1948, p. 1.

[20] *Djalan Baru* p 9; Musso, speech at a PKI rally in Jogja, August 22, reported in *Merdeka*, August 24, 1948, p. 1.

[21] *Djalan Baru,* p. 24 Cf. also *Usui Kompromi Mesti Ditolak*, p. 20; "Pernjataan Mr. Amir Sjarifuddin," *Santapan Rakjat* (I, 102), September 11, 1948, p. 2; declaration of the Socialist Party on entering the PKI, *Merdeka*, September 1, 1948, p. 1; Suripno; in a speech to the BKPRI on August 14, reported in *Merdeka*, August 17, 1948, p. 2; Musso, speech to students in *Jogja*, reported in *Merdeka*, September 7, 1948, p. 1.

[22] Cf John Coast, Recruit to Revolution (London, 1952), pp. 187, 210-215.

stands Soviet Russia,"[23] It can easily be understood that, in. a country which had its back against the wall and was sorely disillusioned with the Western powers, such an argument might have considerable appeal.

Armed with this program for the Indonesian revolution, the Communists now set out to organize a National Front movement which would serve as the mass base supporting their demands on the government. At the same time, they offered to negotiate with the other parties for the forming of a "National Front" cabinet, in which all major political groupings would take part. It was far too late, however, for any compromise between the Communist and pro-government forces, least of all on Communist terms. We shall not go into the details of the events leading up to the complete breakdown of relations between the Communists and the Republican government, save to remark that on September 18 pro-Communist troops in the city of Madiun, under government orders to demobilize, revolted and declared a National Front government. Musso and some of the other PKI leaders, on a tour to propagandize the National Front, immediately went to Madiun and declared against the Jogja government. The rebellion was disorganized, and within a month it had been put down by the government forces; its leaders were either killed in the fighting or executed.

The Indonesian government has claimed that the revolt had been planned by Musso from the beginning; the PKI has maintained that it was provoked by the government, which was bent on crushing the Communists. The truth of the matter may never be known in view of the paucity of documents and unpartisan views on the subject, and it is anyway beyond the scope of this paper to go into the rather elusive evidence as to the revolt's beginnings; but the writer is inclined to give most credence to the view that the fighting was started by lower-echelon Communist leaders in Madiun who became alarmed at the government's attempts to demobilize their troops and at the growing number of incidents which were sapping Communist strength. The PKI leadership, on hearing of the rebellion, decided that the die was cast and that if they did not join in the struggle the government would dismember their forces piece by piece.[24] As for the actual intentions of the government and

---

[23] Musso, in a speech to a PKI rally in Jogja, August 22; quoted in Merdeka, August 25, 1948, p. 1.

[24] Cf. Kahin, *Nationalism and Revolution*, pp. 284, 294; Henri Alers, *Om een rode of groene merdeka* (n.p., 1956), pp. 188-196. Alers maintains, quite reasonably, that it was probable an eventual revolt

the Communists, it is perhaps sufficient to remark that it was apparent to both before the rebellion that the likelihood of civil war in the near future was exceedingly great; and it would have been foolish for either of them to refrain from making plans for such an eventuality.

had been planned by the Communists to center around Madiun, and that it no doubt seemed better to the PKI leaders to go along with the premature rebellion than to see all their plans collapse.

REPUDIATION OF SUKARNO; ENDORSEMENT OF MAO

In spite of the ominous developments in Indonesia during the late summer of 1948, the August mood of the Soviet press was one of friendship as usual. "The Republic of Indonesia is courageously defending her independence against encroachments by the Dutch behind whom loom the monopolists of Wall Street, eager to gain possession of Indonesia's vast natural wealth," the foreign affairs journal *New Times* reported. "The Soviet representatives in the UN systematically expose the real purpose of the intrigues of the colonial imperialists and invariably support every measure aimed at securing genuine independence for the Indonesian people and the territorial integrity of their Republic."[1] So far, all was right with the Soviet world.

The Russian press did not report the arrival of Musso in Indonesia, and it gave very little publicity to the changes that took place in the Communist Party as a result of his efforts. What coverage was given to Indonesia — TASS had a correspondent in Djakarta and another in The Hague — was devoted to a reporting of the various Dutch sinnings against the Republic and the cause of peace. On August 25, however, *Pravda* reported briefly on the SOBSI conference of three days before, declaring that the labor federation demanded a cabinet which would carry out the National Program; Hatta, the article noted, was considered by the conference to be dealing too closely with the imperialists.

This was the first report unfavorable to the Indonesian government since February 29; but it was not followed by any campaign of criticism and thus is probably not of great significance. On September 2, Pravda remarked the decision to form an enlarged Communist Party composed

---

[1] "The Struggle of the Colonial Peoples," *New Times* (No. 32), August 4, 1948, p. 2.

of the old FDR components; and on September 5 it noted the formation of a new PKI Politburo. Meanwhile, the usual reports on the threat of Dutch aggression were kept up.

If the Soviet Union knew beforehand that the Indonesian Communists were going to fight the Republic's government, it certainly showed ho sign of it publicly. *Izvestia* and *Pravda* did not mention the Republic between September 17 and 25; on the latter day the rebellion was first announced. *Pravda*'s report began as follows: "Numerous and contradictory reports are appearing here (in The Hague(, from which the only clear thing that can be gathered is that the situation in Indonesia has lately become worse." This cautious beginning made, the paper continued:

On West and East Java armed skirmishes between Dutch troops and Indonesian are continuing. At the same time it is reported that in the Republican area a conflict is taking place between the Communists and the rightist "National(ist) Party."

The agency ANP (The Dutch wire service) has transmitted a report from Batavia asserting that The Communists have seized power in a large Republican center in West (sic) Java—the city of Madiun. According to the ANP report", Sukarno, speaking over the radio, called for the arrest of Indonesian Communist Party Secretary General Musso.

The Hague, September 21, 1948 (TASS). Dutch newspapers are publishing accounts of the development of events in Indonesia. According to these reports, the radio station at Madiun yesterday transmitted an appeal by Communist Party leader Musso to the Indonesian people, summoning them to join the battle for the independence of the country.

According to the newspapers' assertion, it was stated in a declaration to the public in Madiun that the Sukarno-Hatta government, which is betraying the national interests of Indonesia, must be removed and replaced by a new government answering to the interests of the people.

The Hague, September 21, 1948 (TASS). It is reported that all communications between Djogjakarta and Madiun have been cut off.

The Hague, September 21, 1948 (TASS). Numerous cablegrams are continuing to arrive from Indonesia, on the basis of which, however, it is impossible to obtain a clear picture of the events taking place there.

It is reported that the police, in compliance with orders from the Hatta government, have arrested two hundred members of democratic organizations in Djogjakarta,, Among the arrested were trade union leaders.[2]

We have presented the entire coverage on Indonesia from the September 22 issue of *Pravda* because it illustrates quite well the tenor of Soviet reporting throughout the rebellion. The accounts were short, confused, and, for Soviet journalistic standards, remarkably cautious, it being constantly reminded that they were second-hand reports and that the situation was too confused for any concrete conclusions to be drawn. In this way Pravda, while it reported news sympathetic to the rebels, did not declare itself openly in support of them, nor did it attack the Hatta government save in a manner which attributed the unfavorable opinion to other sources. Contrary to its treatment in the Dutch Communist press, the rebel government was not referred to by Soviet newspapers as the true government of the Republic. Such abstinence from editorializing is not characteristic of Soviet journalism in general, and it is in striking contrast to the opinion on Sukarno and Hatta expressed throughout 1949 by the Russian press.

On the whole, one receives the impression that Pravda considered the whole matter to be a most untoward development, which it preferred to treat gingerly if at all. *Pravda's* caution cannot be laid entirely to a lack of information, since the Dutch Communist press gave the rebellion detailed coverage and almost immediately took a strong stand in favor of Musso and against the Republican government. We cannot know, of course, whether Soviet public comment on the revolt had any relation to the actual attitude of the Russian government; but it is interesting to note that the USSR did not consider it politic to come out openly in support of the rebellion while it was in progress.

While it was hesitant in expressing its opinion on the Indonesian situation during the revolt, the Soviet press did not completely preserve an attitude of business as usual concerning the Republican government. The first note of the attitude which was to be expressed with increasing virulence in the coming months appeared in *Pravda* on October 15, citing as its source the Dutch Communist newspaper — appropriately enough,

---

[2] *Izvestia's* report on the outbreak of the revolt was the same as that in *Pravda*; it subsequently presented less coverage of Indonesian events than the party newspaper, those reports which did appear being generally the same as those published in *Pravda*. This was true as a rule of *Izvestia's* accounts of the Republic throughout the Indonesian revolution.

since the Dutch Communists were the first outside of Indonesia to take this stand:

The organ of the Communist Party, the newspaper "De Waarheid," writes that at the present time certain influential circles in Washington are placing greater stakes on Hatta than on van Mook and Holland's protege, Abdul Kadir. The large American concern "Fox," the newspaper pointed out, has concluded a contract with the Hatta government in accordance with which the Americans will gain control of the richest sources of raw materials in Indonesia. "The bosses of Wall Street," the newspaper concludes, "figure that they will reach their goal more quickly if they do business with Hatta and not with the Dutch. By its conduct, the Dutch government has made it possible for the American imperialists to gain a firm foothold in Indonesia and in Holland. The Hatta government and the Netherlands have now become putty in America's hands.[3]

This interpretation served to explain the fact that the Republican leaders, while they were tools of imperialism, continued to be at odds with the Dutch.

A whole series of intrigues between the Americans and the "Hatta-Sukarno clique" were discovered in explanation of the defeat of the Left:

(US member of the Good Offices Commission) Graham managed to strike a deal with the Indonesian Right-wing groups — Sukiman and Sjamsuddin, leaders of the Moslem Masjumi Party, and A, K. Gani and Ali Sastroamidjojo, leaders of the Nationalist Party. With the help of backstage machinations the Americans were able to secure the downfall of the government of Amir Sjarifuddin which enjoyed the support of the mass of the Indonesian people.

The Hatta government appeared on the scene. …The aura of mystery surrounding him vanished, however, as soon as he included representatives of the Right-wing nationalist parties in the cabinet and began to negotiate with the American government for a loan. …

Indonesian dissatisfaction with the policy of making deals with the colonizers, pursued by the Hatta government, has latterly assumed the proportions of a popular uprising. The struggle for genuine independence

---

[3]   By one of politics' ironic twists, this view was also expressed by the right-wing Dutch press, particularly after the news of the Fox contract appeared. *Pravda*, in fact, several times quotes Trouw (the organ of the Anti-Revolutionary Party) as an authority on the American influence in the Hatta government.

of the Republic has become the focal point of political life. Treacherous elements are attempting behind the backs of the people to come to terms with the American and Dutch imperialists. But the mass of the Indonesians are determined to carry on the fight against the enslavement of the country, for national independence and liberty. And the struggle continues.[4]

This remained the tenor of Soviet comment on Indonesia for the rest of the Indonesian revolution. The Madiun Affair was referred to as a "provocation" rather than a revolt; it had been crushed, but the Indonesian people would not accept the Hatta-Sukarno version of independence and were continuing the armed struggle for liberty.[5] On a more theoretical level, it was asserted that the Hatta governments suppression of the Leftist movement represented a defection by the bourgeoisie from the revolutionary movement: under American pressure, and afraid of the consequences of a thoroughgoing revolution, the bourgeois nationalists had deserted the popular camp and allied with the imperialists.[6]

The Soviet interpretation of the Madiun revolt left no hint as to what attitude the USSR would take towards the Indonesian question in the UN. Since the Republic was now considered to be in reactionary hands, there was no compelling reason why the Soviet Union should defend it; on the other hand, to abandon the cause would release America from its embarrassment at being forced to appear favorable to the colonial viewpoint. The matter was put to the test soon enough: on December 19, 1948, the Dutch attacked the Republic in the second of their "police actions"; in short order they occupied all of Java and arrested the Republic's leaders. The affair was immediately brought up in the Security Council, where Jakob Malik declared unreservedly that the Dutch attack was an unprovoked aggression and a breach of the international peace.[7] The US-

---

[4] G. Afrin, "In Indonesia," *New Times* (No. 45), November 3, 1948, pp. 30-32. Cf. also Berezhkov, "In Indonesia," *New Times*, January 1, 1949, pp. 8-9; Steklov, "Imperialist Aggression in Indonesia," *New Times*, November 16, 1949, p. 6.

[5] Cf. K. Gavrilov, "Rumatsia ustoi imperializma v koloniakh," *Bloknot Agitatora* (No. 24), August 1949, p. 46; V. Ia. Vasil'eva, *Natsional'no-osvoboditel'naia bor'ba v stranakh Iugo-Vostochnoi Azii*, (Moscow, 1949), p. 22.
    This sympathy for all manifestations of continuing conflict led the Soviet Union eventually to praise the activities of some movements whose policies were otherwise far removed from those of Communism — such as the Moslem terrorist Darul Islam. (Cf. *Izvestia*, January 15, 1950).

[6] Cf. *Pravda*, December 26, 1948; I. L. Khaliuta, *Indoneziia* (Moscow, 1949), pp. 11-13.

[7] Cf. also *Pravda*, January 19, 1948.

sponsored resolution on the attack was, he considered, not strong enough. The Russians, it seemed, were prepared to ignore the untoward events of the past months when it came to the UN and world propaganda.

On the whole, the Communists could look back on 1948 as a year in which their ambitions had been checked in the West, while in the East the revolutionary outlook had considerably brightened. The Indonesian Communists had come to a sad if temporary end, but this was more than compensated for by the imminent Communist conquest of China and the active Communist rebellions in Viet Nam, Burma, and Malaya. Clearly, it was high time for a renewed Russian interest in the possibilities of the Asian situation and the development of a uniform theoretical line towards it.

In June a joint session of the Learned Councils of the Institute of Economics and the Pacific Institute of the USSR Academy of Sciences was held to discuss the problem of the national-liberation movement in the colonial and dependent countries.[8]Here at last a unified and detailed analysis of the Asian situation was worked out. Since the conclusions reached here were to form the theoretical background of Soviet policy towards the colonial question for the next few years, we shall give a fairly detailed outline of their content.

The reports presented at the June conference showed a decision to abandon the classical theory of the united front from below and to adopt the assumptions of the Maoist line. That is not to say that the Chinese theory was taken over unaltered; the "National Front" urged here was clearly a Russian view of the Chinese way.

The general theoretical outline was provided by E. M. Zhukov, who reviewed the development of the Asian situation in the postwar period in the light of the new doctrine. Since World War II, Zhukov declared, "American imperialism, heading the anti-democratic camp and aspiring

---

[8]   A report of the proceedings of the conference was published in the October issue of the foreign affairs journal *Voprosi Ekonomiki* ("Narodno-osvoboditel'naia bor'ba v kolonial'nikh i polukolonial'nikh stranakh posle vtoroi mirovoi voini," *Voprosi Ekonomiki* (No. 10, 1949). The major reports presented at the meeting were also reprinted in *Voprosi Ekonomiki* during the fall of 1949 and, in somewhat revised form, appeared in a book issued that year (*krisis kolonial'noi sistemi*, Izdatel'-stvo Akademii Nauk SSSR, Moscow, 1949). Most of the articles in the latter book were translated into English and published by the Indian Communist Party as *Crisis of the Colonial System. The National Liberation Struggle of the Peoples of East Asia* (People's Publishing House, Bombay, 1951); unfortunately , the report on Indonesia was not among those included in the translation, which concerned itself mostly with parts of Asia formerly under British rule.

to world domination, has become the *leader* of the colonial powers, the chief gendarme,… (and thus has) attempted to defeat the national-liberation struggle in all the colonies and semi-colonies."[9] Since the rapid growth of the independence movement made it impossible for the imperialist powers to maintain their policy of direct rule, they made a bid for the support of feudal and landlord interests. They were successful not only in achieving this but also in winning to their side the national bourgeoisie, which had become alarmed at the mass character of the national-liberation movement. Bourgeois nationalism and its offspring, neutralism, were thus enemies of the popular movement in the East:

Bourgeois nationalism in the colonies and semi-colonies has already procured the support of the masses under the ideological-political leadership of the grande bourgeoisie in the majority of the colonial countries which have gone over to the imperialist camp. Bourgeois nation-ism is especially directed against the affiliation of the people's liberation movement in the colonial and dependent countries with the anti-imperialist, democratic camp. …

Similar to the development in the capitalist countries of an attempt by the right socialist betrayers of the working class to spread the rotten notion of the possibility of some sort of "third," middle, road between communism and capitalism, which fallacy in fact serves the forces of imperialist reaction, which are plotting a war against the USSR and the people's democracies, the national-reformists in the colonial and semi-colonial countries are deceitfully chanting about their wish to "stand aside" from the struggle of the two camps, about their "neutrality" as regards what they call the "ideological conflict" between the USSR and the USA, while actually, allied with the reactionary bourgeoisie, they slander the USSR and actively help the imperialists.[10]

In spite of these dire developments, the desertion of the revolutionary cause by the national bourgeoisie has brought one great advantage, for it has placed the leadership of the independence movement in the hands

---

[9] E. Zhukov, "Voprosi natsional'no-kolonial1noi bor'bi posle vtoroi mirovoi voini," *Voprosi Ekonomiki* (No. 9), September 1949, p. 56.

[10] Zhukov, *Voprosi natsional'no-osvoboditel'noi borbi*, pp. 57-58; cf. also G. V. Astaf'eV, "Ot polukolonii k narodnoi demokratii," *Krizis kolonial'noi sistemi*, pp. 82-83; V. Vasil'eva, "Leninsko-stalinskoe uchenie o natsiiakh i natsional'no-kolonial'noi revoliutsii," *Voprosi Ekonomiki* (No. 12), December 1949, p. 104; V. Balabushevich, "Novii etap natsional'-no-osvoboditel'noi bor'bi narodov Indii," *Voprosi Ekonomiki* (No. 8), August 1949, p. 44.

of the proletariat, which is the only class capable of successfully and consistently leading the colonial liberation struggle. It means, moreover, that control of the newly independent state will not be in the hands of the bourgeoisie, with a resulting bourgeois-democratic regime, but will belong to the masses, so that a people's democracy can be directly established: "The leading role of the proletariat in the anti-imperialist struggle, as well as old and recent — postwar — historical experience, combining to unmask completely bourgeois democracy's incapability of guaranteeing the achievement of complete independence and its failure to carry out effective democratic reforms, gave the national-liberation movement the character of a struggle not for bourgeois democracy but for a people's democracy."[11]

If the bourgeoisie could not lead the revolution, it might usefully contribute to it, however, for considerable elements of that class sympathized with the anti-colonial revolt: both the petty bourgeoisie and the national bourgeoisie were potential allies of the workers in this respect.[12] The revolutionary movement in the East could thus be organized on a broader basis than in the capitalist countries:

In the East, in the colonial and semi-colonial countries, it is naturally possible to have a broader National Front against the imperialist forces than in the West. It can without doubt include those sections of the bourgeoisie which are suffering from the ruination of local industry as a result of the dumping of goods from the metropolis. However, the basis of this front is the same as that in European countries: that is, the bloc of working classes — the proletariat, the peasantry, and the urban petty bourgeoisie — under the leadership of the proletariat.

The struggle for a new, popular democracy in the East has its own peculiar features, reflecting the particular nature of the colonial countries in which it takes place. Insofar as the colonial and semi-colonial countries are concerned, a tremendous number of problems of a bourgeois-democratic nature, demanding immediate consideration, stands before the people's democratic authorities. Consequently, the victory of the

---

[11] Zhukov, *Voprosi natsional 'no-osvoboditel 'noi bor'bi*, p. 59. Cf. also Zhukov, "Obostrenie krizisa kolonial'noi sistemi posle vtoroi mirovoi voini," *Krizis kolonial'noi sistemi*, p. 23; Astaf'ev, *Ot polukolonii*, pp. 82-83; "Narodno-osvoboditel'naia bor'ba v kblonial'nikh stranakh posle vtoroi mirovoi voini," *Voprosi Ekonomiki* (No, 10), October 1949, p. 93; Vasil'eva, *Leninsko-stalinskoe uchenie*, p. 118.

[12] Zhukov, *Voprosi natsional'no-osvoboditel'noi* bor'bi, p. 59; Balabushevich, Novii etap, p. 47.

people's democracy in the colonies and dependent countries cannot immediately lead to the tackling of socialist tasks on the scale that this is taking place in the people's democracies in Europe.[13]

The prototype for an Asian people's democracy of the type envisaged above was, according to this theory, Communist China.[14]

It is apparent from the above outline of the argument presented at the June conference that the chief concern of the Soviet analysis of the Chinese revolution centered about the role of the bourgeoisie rather than the peasantry, though most non-Communist observers would probably credit the latter group with far more importance in securing Mao's victory. The fact that the peasantry was an extremely important ally of the proletariat was acknowledged by the Russians, and land reform was considered a major aim of the national liberation movement; but the role of the peasantry did not seem to form a central theoretical question. Possibly the Soviet theoreticians were influenced in this by the general Marxist tendency to discount the peasantry as an active revolutionary force; perhaps, too, they felt that any considerable emphasis on the Chinese Communist handling of the agrarian question at that time would be unpolitic in view of the then current collectivization drive in East Europe. Nor must we forget that the Soviet analysts could not deny the dogma of the revolutionary leadership of the proletariat: to give the peasantry the role it deserved in the Chinese revolution would have been to destroy the theory on which the legitimacy of Communist rule was based. The Chinese Communists themselves seemed to share this feeling, for, as their prospects of victory increased, so did their emphasis on the leading role of the proletariat.

This may do something to explain the lack of emphasis on the peasantry; but we are still confronted with the relative importance granted the bourgeoisie, In dealing with this question it would be well to keep in mind the thesis, introduced earlier in this paper, that the Soviet discussion of the national bourgeoisie was at heart a translation into Marxist terms of the problem of nationalism. Since for the Communists all ideologies are the expressions of class interest, there had to be an

---

[13] Zhukov, E. M., *Obostrenie krizisa kolonial'noi sistemi*, p. 23. Cf. also Zhukov, *Voprosi natsional'no-osvoboditel'noi bor'bi*, p. 60; Vasil'eva, *Leninsko-stalinskoe uchenie*, p. 119.

[14] Zhukov, *Voprosi natsional'no-osvoboditel'noi bor'bi*, pp. 60-61; Cf. also Astaf'ev, *Ot polukolonii*, pp. 82-85; Vasil'eva, *Leninsko-stalinskoe uchenie*, p. 116; Balabushevich, *Novii etap*, p. 39

economic group whose interests were served by nationalism and in terms of which the Communist response to Asian nationalism should be formulated. The Chinese had demonstrated that the Communists themselves could become the spokesmen for nationalism; this was explained in terms of Communist theory by claiming that in the colonial revolution the Communist-led front represented the interests not only of the proletariat but also of the native bourgeoisie struggling against foreign competition. The Soviet emphasis on the national bourgeoisie reflects, according to this theory, a recognition of the importance of nationalism in the Asian revolution and, finally, an acceptance of the Chinese analysis of the Communists' role in regard to it. Just where the theory was merely a justification in terms of Communist doctrine for a phenomenon seen differently on the practical level and where, on the other hand, it actually formed the basis for practical decisions is not generally clear; but it would be difficult to suppose that the dogma could be kept so separate from actual policy discussions as to have had no influence on them. The substitution of a class interest for nationalism obviously presents considerable opportunity for distortion and over-simplification; but such pitfalls are all too often the price of a system which seeks to explain man in terms of a single principle, and Communism has certainly not been free from them.

The report on the Indonesian situation, delivered at the June 1949 Academy of Sciences conference by A. A. Guber, a long-time Indonesia expert and one of the leading figures in the Academy's Pacific Institute, is worthy of some special attention here. Essentially, it is a discussion of the revolution from the point of view of the new Soviet doctrine; and as such it contains a criticism of the PKI's policies during that period. Since the failings of Communist parties are usually conveniently forgotten in Soviet accounts of the world situation, the report's outspokenness makes it one of the major Soviet documents on Indonesia. Briefly, Guber's criticism of the PKI's past policies is this:

The Indonesian Communist Party, though it had gained in prestige through its leading role in the anti-Japanese under-ground, lost control of the revolution to the bourgeoisie, largely because of a lack of available Communist leadership. The Left's position was strengthened by the formation of the Socialist Party under Sjarifuddin and the Labor Party under Setiadjit at the end of 1945, but this in itself was a tactical error, since there should have been but one party representing the Communist point of view. (Guber, of course, takes the stand that Setiadjit and Sjarifuddin were Communists at the time.)

The Communists took a conciliatory attitude regarding relations with the Dutch and approved the Linggadjati Agreement, on the theory that this would give them a breathing space in which to strengthen the Republics position. This shows, Guber argued, that the PKI did not have an adequate knowledge of imperialist tactics after World War II; in fact, much of their faith in the workability of the Linggadjati compromise was based on a belief that the Philippines had actually been granted complete independency by the United States. Only the right wing — the Masjumi and the PNI — opposed the agreement; and they did so because they were tools of the American imperialists, who were aiming at securing Indonesia for themselves.

Another serious mistake on the part of the Indonesian Communists was their Refusal to participate openly as a party in the first three Republican governments and their assumption of a very minor post in the Sjarifuddin cabinet: the Communists should have gained a firm grip on the governmental machinery, and once having obtained it should have refused to let go. The PKI did not differentiate its policies sufficiently from those of other Indonesian movements, and even when the Sjarifuddin government was in power no major reform measures were taken. The Left thus failed to secure itself either in the bureaucracy or among the masses.

Meanwhile, the Americans had come to see in the Indonesian nationalist movement a means of replacing Dutch economic control over Indonesia with their own. That the Left did not see through the US machinations and was persuaded to approve the Renville Agreement was a sign of its inexperience in political affairs and the influence of the petty-bourgeois element that existed in the Left Wing. The rightist nationalists, too, began to see in American an alternative to the two horns of their dilemma — the Left and the Dutch. The Communists, however, failed to point out to the masses the Right's loss of revolutionary fervor, a mistake which hindered the fight for the unification of the people and weakened leftist influence on the masses. Even after the fall of the Sjarifuddin government, the left wing did not sufficiently differentiate itself from the government's policies. Although it criticized the Hatta regime and demanded another cabinet, it took no important steps that might displease the government, since it did not desire a permanent alienation from the Right.

All these mistakes were not corrected until the late summer of 1948, when, driven by the reactionary policies of the Hatta government, the leftist parties united in an enlarged PKI and began to expose the iniquity of the Right, By then it was too late, however; the Hatta government responded with police measures which could only be answered by revolt. Since the previous weak policy of the Communists had left the populace unprepared to take arms against the government, and since the uprising was badly organized, the revolt was easily crushed by the forces of reaction.[15]

A biased viewpoint, to say the least, Its main interest for us is that it is in its main points the same criticism of the PKI's past policies as that given by Musso a year before. Indeed, if we compare the doctrine presented at the June conference with the policies propounded by Musso, we can see a remarkable similarity. Again, we may speculate whether the Soviet policy-makers, on outlining a policy for their emissary to Indonesia, chose in favor of the version of Maoism which the Soviet Union was developing but had not yet quite accepted.

A day after the opening of the Academy of Sciences conference, *Pravda* undertook the publication in full of Liu Shao-chi's *Internationalism and Nationalism*,[16]a work setting forth the Chinese view on the nationalist question and pointing out the importance of an "anti-imperialist alliance with that section of the national bourgeoisie which is still opposing imperialism and which does not oppose the anti-imperialist struggle of the masses of the people. Should the Communists fail to do so in earnest,

---

[15] A. A. Cuber, "Indoneziiskii narod v bor'be za nezavisimost," *Krizis kolonial'noi sistemi*, pp. 151-177. A minor item — but of curiosity in view of the present Communist feud with the Islamic party — is Guber's assertion, referring to the Indonesian situation in 1947, that it would have been possible for the Communists to infiltrate the Masjumi: "The parties of the left bloc had a significant opportunity to broaden their influence within the larger Moslem party — the Masjumi, Although the leadership of this party represented the more conservative wing in the Republican camp, and its leaders, particularly Agus Salim, had shown themselves even before the war to be capitulators to Dutch imperialism, the mass membership consisted of peasants, craftsmen, and petty bourgeoisie." As for the PNI: "Up to a certain time the petty bourgeois part of the leadership of the National Party, and even its unofficial leader — President Sukarno — not only did not hinder the activities of the left bloc, but to a significant degree relied on its support against the rightist elements in the Masjumi and in the National Party itself." (pp 162-163) This did not, however; prevent Guber from taking as unfriendly a view towards Sukarno as did the general line of Soviet comment after the Madiun Affair.

[16] June 7, 8, and 9, 1949. Cf. Kautsky *Moscow and the Communist* Party of India, p. 175.

should they, to the contrary, oppose or reject such an alliance, it would also constitute a grave mistake. Such an alliance must be established in all sincerity even if it should be of an unreliable, temporary and unstable nature"[17]

Following this, a rash of articles by Chinese and on the Chinese revolution appeared in the Soviet and Cominform publications. Whereas the keynote message at the 1948 anniversary of the October revolution had contained no mention of China in its survey of the Asian situation,[18]the 1949 speech devoted its Asian section entirely to the accomplishments of the Chinese Communist Party: "Under the tried guidance of its leader Mao Tsi-tung (*tumultuous applause*), it organized and rallied workers, peasants, intellectuals, and all the patriotic forces of the nation…The victory of Chinese democracy opens a new page not only in the history of the Chinese people, but also in that of all the peoples of Asia, the Pacific and of the entire colonial world, has reached a new and considerably higher level. The triumph of democracy in China signifies a serious strengthening of the positions of the world democratic anti-imperialist camp fighting *for a lasting peace*."[19]

The high mark of Chinese prestige came in November, when the Communist-dominated World Federation of Trade Unions held a conference of Asian and Australasian countries in Peking. There Liu Shao-chi declared in the keynote address that "The course followed by the Chinese people in defeating imperialism and its lackeys and in founding the People's Republic of China is the course that should be followed by the peoples of the various colonial and semi-colonial countries in their fight for national independence and people's democracy[20]And he went on to explain the Chinese concept of a broad anti-imperialist front, led by the Communists and, contrary to the neutralists, whom he roundly denounced, leaning towards the Soviet camp.

---

[17] Liu Shao-chi, *Nationalism and Internationalism* (Peking, n.d.), p. 47. The pamphlet, was first published in December 1948.

[18] V. K. Molotov, "31st Anniversary of the Great October Socialist Revolution," Report at a Celebration Meeting of the Moscow Soviet, November 6, 1948, *For a Lasting Peace* (No. 22), November 15, 1948, p. 3.

[19] G. M. Malenkov, "Thirty-second Anniversary of the Great October Socialist Revolution," Report delivered at the anniversary meeting of the Moscow Soviet, November 6, 1949, *For a Lasting Peace* (No. 26), November 11, 1949, p. 2.

[20] "The Trade Union Conference of Asian and Australasian Countries," *World Trade Union Movement* (WFTU journal), (No. 8), December 1949, p. 14.

The apparently complete endorsement of the Chinese line by the Soviet Union at the end of 1949 was to be considerably qualified in the following years. Probably the USSR, having gotten over its first admiration for the Chinese Communist victory, had some second thoughts on the advisability of praising too highly a potential rival for Asian Communist allegiance. Again, a growing Soviet appreciation of the force of nationalism probably contributed to the lessening insistence that the Asian Communists reiterate publicly their loyalty to Moscow or Peking.

The theory itself also underwent a change, as the USSR began to realize that Asian neutralism could work to its own advantage. The question was now no longer one of Communist victory in an Asian revolution, but of the relationship of Communist parties to bourgeois nationalist governments whose friendship the Soviet Union desired. Obviously, the principle of Communist hegemony over the nationalist movement, which the USSR had seen in the beginning as the most important contribution of the Chinese experience, had no place here. National interest fought with ideology, and, as is usual in politics, national interest won out. More and more the all-inclusive, nationalist aspect of the National Front was emphasized, the need for Communist hegemony toned down; so that the present day Communist line for Asia bears very little resemblance to the militant dogma of 1949.

Things had not gone this far by the end of the Indonesian revolution, however. After long and weary quarrelings in The Hague, Indonesia's independence was conceded by the Dutch on December 27, 1949. The Soviet Union immediately recognized the Republic, but made it quite clear that the USSR did not approve of the new nation's rulers:

The first steps taken by the so-called "government" of Hatta-Sukarno after the Hague deal prove that this clique is ready to serve its real masters- — the American imperialists — faithfully and well. Feverish military preparations on the part of the imperialists and their parasites have been brought about by the fact that they have not succeeded in deceiving the Indonesian people by the false "self-determination" which Indonesia received in The Hague, and (The people) are continuing the struggle for their genuine independence.[21]

---

[21] *Izvestia*, January 15, 1950.

On this cheerful note, the Soviet Union took up relations with an independent Indonesia. It would be a long time before Sukarno would be a welcome visitor to Moscow.

INDEX

This book is indexed using Google Book Search.
Kindly visit books.google.com and enter in the title or ISBN.

www.ingramcontent.com/pod-product-compliance
Lightning Source LLC
Chambersburg PA
CBHW020006290326
41935CB00007B/330